CW00855436

Motorway Walks

Short countryside walks within five miles of UK motorway exits, with dog-friendly pubs and cafes.

Sold in aid of ....

Border Collie Trust GB

www.bordercollietrustgb.org.uk
Reg. Charity No. 1053585

Thank you for your support !!!

Motorway Walks

Short countryside walks within five miles of UK motorway exits, with dog-friendly pubs and cafes.

Researched and written by Lezli and David Rees

A CIP catalogue record for this book is available from the British Library

The contents of this book are believed correct at the time of printing. Nevertheless the authors cannot be held responsible for any errors or omissions or for changes in the details given in this book or for the consequences of any reliance on the information it provides. This does not affect your statutory rights. We have tried to ensure accuracy in the book, but things do change and we would be grateful if readers would advise us of any inaccuracies they may encounter.

We have taken care to ensure that these walks are safe. The authors accept no responsibility for any injuries caused to readers whilst following these walks.

Updates and corrections are posted to the authors' website at www.drivingwithdogs.co.uk

ISBN: 978-1-4092-8586-1

The Motorways

Anyone who drives on the motorways will benefit from this guide to walks within 5 miles of motorway exits. All the UK is covered, from Exeter to Perth and Swansea to Canterbury.

Use this book to get more fun for your petrol, see more of the countryside, take a healthy break, or to enjoy a relaxing pub lunch.

Each page features a 30 to 45 minute walk, with a selected pub or café on the walk. Activities for children are included, from bouncy castles to nature trails.

All the walks are suitable for dogs. People with assistance dogs will find details of accessible paths and disabled facilities. The listed pubs all welcome well-behaved dogs.

Most of the pubs are traditional inns, serving high quality food at realistic prices. Landlords, chefs and opening times can change quickly, and phone numbers are given for you to check in advance to avoid disappointment.

Over 500 more motorway walks, dog-friendly pubs, beaches and country walks are on our website: www.drivingwithdogs.co.uk. We hope you visit the site and share your comments and suggestions.

M1

From London to Leeds, via Leicester and Sheffield

Junction

WD6 3AT Aldenham Country Park

Getting there

From Junction 5 take the A41 Harrow, northbound exit 1, southbound exit 2. At a roundabout take exit 2, Central London A41, past a McDonalds on the left. At the next roundabout take exit 1, Aldenham Country Park. Turn left, Aldenham Road. Turn left to the car park.

Return to M1 Junction 5

Turn right from car park, Aldenham Road. Continue to the A41 junction and turn left, Aylesbury. At the roundabout take exit 2, A41 signed M1 and return to the motorway.

Walk

For a 30-40 minute stroll, walk through the car park, away from the adventure playground and farm, following signs to the 100 Aker Wood. The Pooh Bear theme expands and you can visit the 'homes' of Kanga, Eeyore and Wol. There's an enclosed paddock for dogs to run free.

A longer 40-60 minute circular Lakeside Walk starts from the refreshment kiosk.

The urban farm is well worth a visit, with or without children, with a collection of farmyard favourites including an enormous grinning sow, leaping goats, shire horses and rare-breed sheep.

Facilities

Car park: weekdays £4.00, weekends and holidays £5.00, cash only. WC, refreshment kiosk, picnic area, adventure playground, urban farm. Campervan access.

Brickett Wood Common *AL2 3XU*

Getting there

Southbound: turn right, signed North Watford.
Northbound: exit onto A405N St Albans. Take a sharp right at A405N. Take the M1 exit signed North Watford.
Continue on Mount Pleasant Lane over two mini-roundabouts. Drive under a railway bridge and turn immediately right, School Lane. Continue to The Old Fox car park.

Return to M1 Junction 6

Return up School Lane, turn left onto Mount Pleasant Lane. Then turn right onto Hunters Ride, and left, Black Boy Wood. Turn right onto South Riding, then right into West Riding and quickly left onto Oakwood Road. At the end of Oakwood Road turn left at the A405, North Watford, and rejoin the M1 as signed.

Walk

This area is an unspoilt byway that remains rooted in the life of a century ago.
Start the walk across the road from the Old Fox and enter the wood at a public footpath sign. Ramble on the paths inside the wood, there is no particular route here.

Facilities

At The Old Fox. Bar snacks/food available. Well-behaved dogs permitted in the bar and garden area. Dog water provided. Campervan access.

Getting there
From Junction 8 merge onto the A414, Hemel Hempstead.
At the next roundabout take exit 2, A414. At the next roundabout take exit 1, A4147 St Albans. Pass a pub and turn right signed Bedmond (Bedmond Road). Continue to Pimlico and park at The Swan on the left hand side. Non-patrons may use the car park with permission.

Return to M1 Junction 8
Turn right, Bedmond Road, and continue to the T-junction to turn left at the A4147, signed Hemel Hempstead. At the roundabout take the A414, signed M1, Hatfield and the North to return to the M1.

Walk
From the car park turn left onto the road. After a few metres turn right up some steps at a public footpath sign.
After a 10 minute walk on a broad fenced path between fields enter a large field. Continue with the hedgerow to the left. Notice a wireless station beyond the hedge to the left and just after this is a waymark. Continue straight, and admire the spectacular views. This path leads to Hyde Farm, which is a good place to turn around and retrace your steps to The Swan.

Facilities
The Swan (01923 263093) is open all day. Bar food and snacks served. Outside seating and children's play area. Well-behaved dogs are welcome at this traditional 16th century pub.

M1 Junction 11

Dunstable Downs Country Park

Getting there

From Junction 11 take the A505, Dunstable, northbound exit 1, southbound exit 3. At the next roundabout take exit 2, Dunstable A505. Pass a BP garage on the left and a retail park (with Sainsbury and McDonalds) to the right. In Dunstable, follow signs to Aston Clinton B489, over 3 mini roundabouts. At the next roundabout turn left, Whipsnade B4541, and continue to the Dunstable Downs car park on the right. The second car park is close to the facilities and café.

Return to M1 Junction 11

Turn left from the car park and turn right, signed B489 Dunstable. Stay on the B489 through Dunstable and continue straight as the B489 becomes the A505, signed M1 and Luton.

Walk

Starting from the visitor centre, first enjoy the view from this astonishing vantage point overlooking the Chiltern Valley. The walk follows part of the Icknield Way, an ancient track that was the pre-Roman highway between the Ivinghoe Beacon in Hertfordshire and Norfolk. It's one of the oldest known routes in Britain, and there is more detail on the notice board. Follow the clearly signed path and turn round to return at your halfway point.

Facilities

P&D car park, NT members free. WC+disabled, visitor centre, café, shop. Campervan access.

Getting there

From Junction 12 follow signs to Flitwick/Woburn A5120.
At the roundabout take exit 2, Harlington Station. Pass the railway station. At the crossroads turn right, past The Carpenters Arms, and continue to the brow of the hill where the car park is on the left.

Return to M1 Junction 12

Turn right out of the car park. Turn left at the crossroads just after The Carpenters Arms. Pass Harlington Station on the left, and then turn left onto Toddington Road. At the roundabout take exit 1, A5120 Harlington Road and rejoin the motorway.

Walk

Sundon Hills is one of the highest points in Bedfordshire, with stunning views over the county and the Sharpenhoe Clappers. The long distance John Bunyan Trail passes through the park. There are no marked paths, but the rolling hills are grassy and easy to navigate. It's easy to see why Sundon Hills is part of the Chilterns Area of Outstanding Natural Beauty.

Facilities

Free parking. Wheelchair access. Picnic tables. Campervan access.
At The Carpenters Arms (01525 872384). Meals and snacks Tues-Sun 1200-2300, Mon 1800-2200. Well-behaved dogs are welcome in the bar.

M1 Junction 14

Broughton Grounds Community Woodlands

Getting there

From Junction 14, take the A509 Milton Keynes. At the next roundabout take A5130, Woburn Sands/Wavendon. Turn left, signed Gravel Quarry/Broughton Grounds Lane – no through road. Pass a riding school on the right, go over the motorway and the entrance to the small car park is on the left on a right hand corner.

Return to M1 Junction 14

Retrace your route, turning right at the end of Broughton Grounds Lane.

Walk

From the car park take the track on the right, going through a gate, until you see a yellow waymark. Follow the arrow direction into the field ahead. About half way across the field turn right and pass a pond to the left. Continue to the waymarked footbridge and stile and then turn half-right into a newly planted wood. At a crossing of paths, continue straight on to a gate.

A fishing lake will be on the right. Follow the path along the left side of the field and back to the car park.

In the woodland section you may well see Muntjac deer. These are the smallest deer in the UK, and not aggressive.

Facilities

Free parking. Campervan access.

Salcey Forest

Getting there

From Junction 15 take the A508 Stony Stratford at the first roundabout, and then exit 2 at the next roundabout. Enter Roade and turn left onto Northampton Road. Pass a school on the left and turn left, signed Hartwell. Drive though Hartwell. At the crossroads turn left signed Quinton, Northampton. Salcey Forest car park is on the right.

Return to M1 Junction 15

Turn left from the car park, and then turn right, signed Hartwell. Continue through Hartwell village to enter Roade. At the T-junction turn right, signed Northampton. At the next T-junction turn right signed M1 (A508).

Walk

Salcey Forest is a small survivor of a former royal forest, and contains ancient oak trees known as 'druids' that are said to be over 500 years old. With a keen eye, you can still see signs of ancient wood banks and buildings.

There are three marked trails through the woods on well maintained paths. The first trail is 0.75 mile and is suitable for wheelchair users. The second trail is 1.5 miles, and the third trail is 6 miles.

There is plenty for all the family to do, including a Tree-top walk.

Facilities

P&D gated car park £2.00 per day, closes at 1900 in summer. Café, WC, children's play area. Campervan access.

M1 Junction 18

Crick *NN6 7TX*

Getting there

From Junction 18 take the turning signed 'Dept of Transport Weighbridge'. At a roundabout take exit 3, Yelvertoft, Crick. At the next roundabout take exit 1 Crick, Yelvertoft. Enter Crick. Drive to the top of the hill and park near the Red Lion on the right.

Return to M1 Junction 18

Leave the Red Lion and take exit 2 at the roundabout. At the next roundabout take exit 1, A428 Rugby and rejoin the motorway at the next roundabout.

Walk

From the Red Lion turn left. Pass the High Street turning and go down the hill. Turn left, The Derry. At the footpath arrows, follow an arrow to the right. Cross a stile and follow the arrow uphill to another post. Take a half left to carry on over the brow of the hill. Head for a black arrow to the right of a tree and then cross a wooden footbridge and stile into the next field.

Head slightly to the left up the next hill. Climb a stile to the left of a tree to an arrow pointing half left. Over the hill aim for a gap in the far left corner of the field and walk through to the next field. Turn round here and retrace your steps.

Facilities

At the 17th century Red Lion. Food and snacks are available. Dogs are allowed in the bar and beer garden. Campervan access.

Getting there

From Junction 20 take the A304, Market Harborough. Enter Walcote and park at The Tavern Inn on the left.

Return to M1 Junction 20

Turn right out of the car park onto the A4304. This leads directly back to the M1 Junction 20.

Walk

Turn right from the car park and walk to a footpath sign on the other side of the road. Turn right at the gateway of No.5, through the garden and the wooden gate and stile on the other side. Follow an arrow pointing slightly to the right along the bottom of a field. Climb a stile and follow the arrow straight on. Turn left after a children's play area to follow the bridleway to Misterton. Stay on the bridleway through a gate and into a field. Bear left to join a farm track. The track becomes a surfaced lane and crosses a stream. This is the outskirts of Misterton village, with a church on the right. Turn around here to retrace the route to Walcote.

Facilities

At The Tavern Inn, Walcote (01455 553338). Food served 1200-2130. Dogs welcome at the outdoor tables, dog water available. Petrol station in village. Campervan access.

Billa Barra Hill Nature Reserve

Getting there

From Junction 22 take the A511 Ashby, Coalville. Pass a BP service station. At the roundabout take exit 1, Stanton, Thornton. Pass Markfield Equestrian Centre on the left. Turn right, signed Local Nature Reserve, Billa Barra Lane. Take the first right turn for the National Forest car park.

Return to M1 Junction 22

Turn left from the car park. Turn left at the T-junction and continue to a roundabout. Take exit 2 to rejoin the M1.

Walk

Go through the kissing gate at the back of the car park and walk up the hill. Follow the path as it bears to the right beside the Charnwood Noon Column.

Continue towards the trees and gorse bushes, ignoring a path crossing your way. Bear right between holly trees, then bear half left along the clearly trodden path towards the top of the hill, passing through a gap in the hedgerow. Continue with a dry stone wall to the left to the very top of the mound. Walk down the other side and you'll be able to see the car park at the bottom.

Facilities

None on walk.

BP Service station on A511 with Burger King, Little Chef, petrol and WC. Campervan access.

Donington Services

Getting there
Follow signs to Donington Services from Junction 23A.

Return to M1 Northbound
Follow the signs to return to the M1 via the A453.

Walk
This is one of the gateways to the National Forest, with an information board near the services entrance explaining the project.
Keeping the services block on the left, follow a path round to the start of a grassy area. Then walk forward, bearing slightly right, to join a path leading parallel to one of the service roads. Follow this path to the public footpath sign, and then turn left.
At this point, the walk becomes properly rural as the path leads downhill between tilled fields and the sound of the motorway gives way to birdsong. Follow the path for 20 minutes or so, and then turn round to return to the car park.

Facilities
Moto service station, with a Thorntons chocolate shop as well as the usual retail outlets. Dogs on leads may be taken to the outside tables. Campervan access.

Elvaston Country Park *DE72 3EP*

Getting there
From Junction 25 take the A52 Derby, northbound exit 1, southbound exit 4. Enter Borrowash and turn left, Victoria Avenue. At a T-junction turn right. At the next T-junction turn left, and immediately right, Station Road. Turn right at the brown signpost to Elvaston Country Park. This is also the Derby Showground, busy on major show days.

Return to M1 Junction 25
Leave the car park and turn left. Enter Borrowash. Turn left onto the A6005, signed Derby. Enter Spondon. At the roundabout take the 2nd exit and at the next roundabout take the 3rd exit, signed M1 to return to the motorway.

Walk
To join the trails, turn left from the rear of the car park to cross the bridge. Turning to the left takes you through a majestic avenue of Cedars of Lebanon to approach the 'castle' (which is more of a stately home) on a broad grassy approach. The café, visitor centre and shop lie in the courtyard.

There are more than 200 acres of woodland and formal gardens here, so there are many trail options to choose from, all starting from the central courtyard.

Facilities
Car park Mon-Fri £1.50 after 0900; Bank hols and weekends £2.00. WC+disabled, café, shop, visitor centre, easy-access trails, children's playground, nature trails, riding. Free dog poo bags from car park kiosk. Campervan access.

Getting there

From Junction 27 take the A608/A611 signed Hucknall, crossing two roundabouts. At the traffic lights continue towards Hucknall. At the next two roundabouts take exit 1, Linby B6011. After a railway crossing, enter Linby and park in The Horse and Groom car park on the left.

Return to M1 Junction 27

Turn right from the car park and take exit 2, Mansfield, at the roundabout. At the next roundabout, take exit 3 signed Mansfield, M1 and then follow signs to return to the motorway.

Walk

With your back to the Horse and Groom, turn right past the war memorial and at the roundabout turn right at a wooden public footpath sign. This is the Linby Trail, a straight wide path running alongside a brook. After a mile or so the path divides and the path on the right continues up a small hill to the gatehouse for Newstead Abbey, the sometime home of the poet Lord Byron. Reverse the route to return to Linby.

Facilities

The Horse and Groom (0115 963 2219), food and snacks available, roasts on Sundays. Children's play area. Well-behaved dogs permitted in the bar area and garden seating. Café, WC, visitor centre, shop at Newstead Abbey. Campervan access.

M1 Tibshelf Services

Five Pits Trail *DE55 5TZ*

Getting there
Leave the M1 and park at Tibshelf Services.

Return to M1
Return to the M1 from the services as signed.

Walk
Southbound services. Head up the bank from the services vehicle entrance and turn left at the top to follow a trodden path to a fence. Cross the fence and turn left onto a surfaced path and over the motorway bridge. Stay on this path, ignoring other turnings, to the entrance to the trails.
Northbound services. Walk towards the motel and exit on the service road. Turn right, and walk a few yards to a house before a bridge. Turn right here onto a track. Turn left and walk downhill to a bike barrier and the start of the trails.
Both routes now reach a waymark, which shows paths branching off in every possible direction. Turn right onto the Five Pits Trail, just one of many fine walking routes here.

Facilities
RoadChef motorway services, northbound and southbound. Campervan access.

Hardwick Inn and Woods

Getting there

From Junction 29 take the A6175, Clay Cross, Hardwick Hall. Northbound exit 1, southbound exit 4.
Turn left signed Stainsby, Hardwick Hall and Stainsby Mill. Drive under the M1, and take the second left turn signed Hardwick Inn. Park in the overspill car park on the right before the inn.

Return to M1 Junction 29

Reverse your route, the motorway is clearly signed.

Walk

Walk past the pub, around a cattle grid and uphill on the lane. At a footpath sign bear right through a wooden gate. Follow the grassy track straight ahead, through a gate and uphill to a purple waymark for the 'Hardwick Rowthorne Walk'. At the top there's a National Trust board showing routes of the many walks available here. The path to the left leads to Hardwick Hall (open 9-5, and no dogs). Turn right to walk through the woodland (Lady Spencer's Walk).
For a shorter walk, you may decide to forego the marked trails and just enjoy pottering in the woodland.

Facilities

Hardwick Inn (01246 850245). A 15th century coaching inn providing snacks and meals, and a very large garden. Food available 1130 to 2130, Sundays from 12 noon. Dogs welcome outside, water buckets provided. Campervan access.
Hardwick Halls: NT/English Heritage licensed restaurant, and refreshment kiosk in car park. Dogs outside on leads only.

M1 Junction 31

Rother Valley Country Park *S26 5PQ*

Getting there

From Junction 31 take the A57 Sheffield, northbound exit 1, southbound exit 3. At the roundabout take exit 1, A618 signed Rother Valley Country Park. Turn right to the car park.

Return to M1 Junction 31

Exit the park and turn left. At the roundabout take exit 2, A57 Worksop and return to the M1.

Walk

This 750 acre country park has a number of trails and strolling areas. It's also a stunningly brilliant way of making positive use of the town's flood defences – which is what this park is all about. A network of footpaths is clearly signed from the visitor centre, near the WCs and children's activities.

Dog walkers tend to park in one of the earlier lakeside car parks and choose circular routes around the lakes. The first lake, and the smallest, is the Northern Lake which can be walked around in 45 minutes or so. The Rother Valley Lake is the largest one, and this is a much longer walk.

Facilities

Several large car parks. Entry £2.50, includes parking. Closes dusk. WC + disabled, café, shops, visitor centre, craft centre, therapy rooms, PlayDales for children. Campervan access.

S31 0YL — Ulley Country Park

Getting there

From Junction 33 take the A630, Sheffield Centre. Turn left, Catcliffe B6533. At a roundabout take exit 1, Catcliffe B6533, and at the next roundabout, turn to Catcliffe B6066. There is a retail park on this roundabout, with a Morrisons and Burger King.

Follow the road to the left at a quarry entrance, through Catcliffe. Turn right just before a railway bridge, signed Treeton. Pass through Treeton, over a mini roundabout and at the junction turn left, signed Rotherham. Turn right at the sign for Ulley Country Park.

Return to M1 Junction 33

Turn left from the car park, A618. At the junction turn right, Treeton Lane, and turn left by the railway bridge. Follow the road round to the right, and then take exit 2 at the retail park roundabout, and exit 2 at the next roundabout. Take exit 3 at the next roundabout, A630, signed Rotherham/M1 to rejoin the M1.

Walk

Turn left at the lake. Cross the road by the bridge after approx 0.8 mile, and continue along the clearly marked permissive path. This is not a circular route, so you have the option to continue on the marked route for the full 5 miles or so, or to turn round whilst the lake is still in view to return to the visitor centre.

Facilities

P&D car park 30p/50p, WC, information centre (re-opening 2009), drinks machine, free dog poo bags. Campervan access.

Scholes Coppice *S61 2RQ*

Getting there

From Junction 35 take the A629 Rotherham. Enter Thorpe Hesley. Pass a Texaco garage and just after a pub turn left into Scholes Lane. Enter Scholes and park in The Bay Horse car park on the right.

Return to M1 Junction 35

Turn left from the car park. At the crossroads turn right onto the A629 and continue to Junction 35.

Walk

Turn left from the car park and then turn left at a public footpath sign along a driveway. This brings you into Scholes Coppice.

Walk over the footbridge as far as a fork in the path to the footpath signs. The 45 minute circular walk is clearly marked with yellow arrows.

A slight detour, signed, leads to an information board explaining the Iron Age history of the coppice.

Facilities

At the Bay Horse (0114 2468085). The Bay Horse is a traditional inn, with a good selection of hearty bar snacks and meals and a roaring fire in winter. Meals are available weekends from 1200, weekdays from 1700.

Well-behaved dogs on leads are welcome in the rear bar. Campervan access.

Cannon Hall Park

Getting there

From Junction 37 take the A628 Manchester. At the next roundabout take exit 3, Manchester A628, and at the following roundabout take exit 1, Manchester A628. At the next roundabout take exit 2 and bear right to Higham Lane. Continue onto Higham Common Road and at the traffic lights turn left, A635. Turn right, Bark House Lane, at a tourist sign for Cannon Hall Country Park and turn right to the park.

Return to M1 Junction 37

Turn left from the car park, and at the T-junction turn left signed Barnsley A635. At the traffic lights turn right, signed Dodworth. Thereafter follow signs for Barnsley A628 to reach the M1 interchange.

Walk

There's little chance of getting lost in this 70 acre expanse of largely flat and open parkland. Walk alongside the small river from the car park and then strike out into the park on a broad path. Follow the path on a circular orbit for a 30-40 minute walk.

If you have time, the historic walled garden next to the Hall is worth a visit. Quaffers of Australian wine will be intrigued to know that a cutting from a vine cultivated in one of these greenhouses was exported to Australia in 1802 and its offspring form the roots of today's Ozzie wine industry.

Facilities

P&D car park £2.50 disabled free (correct change only), WC+disabled. Café with fresh cakes, home made soup.

Cannon Hall Museum open 1100-1700 Mon-Wed, Sat, Sun. Free entrance.

M1 Junction 38

Yorkshire Sculpture Park

Getting there

From Junction 38 take the A637 Huddersfield. Continue, ignoring a car park on the left, and turn left signed Sculpture Park at a roundabout.

Return to M1 Junction 38

Turn right out of the park onto the A637 and rejoin the M1 at the next roundabout.

Walk

This walk lies in the Yorkshire Sculpture Park, an outdoor art gallery. The gallery reception desk has useful maps of the park and sculptures.

Start from the gate by the gallery to follow the path downhill towards the lake. Bear left at the foot of the slope to walk with the lake on the right. Turn right through a gate onto Dam Head bridge to join the marked Longside Route around the perimeter of the park in a full circle past the Longside gallery. Turn right after the bridge to keep the lake on the right to return to the car park. Watch out for territorial geese by the lake.

Facilities

P&D £4.00. Open Winter 10-5, Summer 10-6. WC+disabled, café, gallery, gallery shop. Free walks leaflets. Dog water provided. Outdoor seating by café where dogs are permitted. Campervan access.

Pugneys Country Park

Getting there
From Junction 39 take the A636, Wakefield. At the roundabout take exit 2, A636 Wakefield. At the next roundabout take exit 3 into Pugneys Country Park.

Return to M1 Junction 39
Leave the park, take exit 2 at the roundabout, Denby Dale A636/M1. At the next roundabout, take exit 2 signed M1/A636 to return to the M1.

Walk
The main purpose of this park is to encourage water sports in the area, and two fine lakes and a nature reserve have been created from the sites of former quarries and open cast mines.
The lakes are surrounded with 250 acres of grassland, making this a soft and gentle walking landscape.
A surfaced and accessible 1.6 mile circular path runs around the larger lake, ideal for a 45 minute walk. It can get very exciting to watch the dinghy sailors and surfers in training on a windy day as you walk.

Facilities
Free parking. Car park 0900-2130. WC, Café, picnic tables, children's play area. Petrol station on the A636. Campervan access.

Temple Newsam *LS15 0AE*

Getting there
From Junction 46 take the A63 Leeds. At the next roundabout take exit 3, A6120, ring road. Follow the A6120 at the next roundabout. At the third roundabout take exit 2, A63 and Temple Newsam House. At the traffic lights turn left signed Temple Newsam House, Colton Road. Go straight over a mini-roundabout into Temple Newsam.

Return to M1 Junction 46
Leave the Lodge car park, turn left to return on Colton Road to the traffic lights on the Selby Road. Turn right (A63) and then take exit 2 at the roundabout, signed M1.

Walk
With over 1,500 acres of woodland and parkland there is plenty of walking choice. There are thirty distinct woods within the grounds, as well as a number of different gardens. From the house, a pleasant circular walk goes past Little Temple to Wilderness Wood, onward to Coppice Wood and back to the house via Pegasus Wood.
Dog walkers may prefer to start at the Lodge car park, and walk over the gently undulating velvet green grass towards the house and then into the woods.

Facilities
The Lodge car park, free.
House car park P&D £3.60. Visitor centre (0113 264 7321), WC+disabled, tea rooms, shop. Campervan access.

M2

From London to Canterbury, via Chatham

Junction

M2 Junction 1

Westbound only

Shorne Wood *DA12 3HX*

Getting there

From Junction 1 continue forward onto the A2. Take the Cobham, Shorne exit, and then exit 1 at a roundabout, Brewers Road. Continue ahead, then turn left into Shorne Wood Country Park.

Return to A2 westbound

Turn right out of the car park, and at the roundabout take exit 4, signed London M25, to rejoin the A2 westbound.

Walk

Shorne Wood is over 170 acres of ancient woodland and heath, water meadows and lakes. It was formerly part of the Cobham Estate.

There are several colour-coded paths and circular walks that lead out of the park. A guide leaflet is available for these routes at the information centre.

The Woodland Track, which starts at the visitor centre, provides a very dog-centred walk. There's a sign pointing to Shorne Cam pool – a designated venue for dog swimming.

Facilities

P&D parking. WC+disabled, visitor centre, café, shop, picnic area, sensory garden, recycle bins, adventure playground. Electro-scooter hire, book on 01474 823800. Campervan access.

Ranscombe Park Nature Reserve

Getting there

From Junction 2 take the A228 Rochester, West Malling. At the next roundabout take exit 2 signed M20, West Malling. The small car park for Ranscombe Park is immediately on the right.

Return to M2 Junction 2

Leave the car park, turn left and join the motorway at the roundabout.

Walk

Several trails are indicated by yellow waymarks, and the North Downs Way also passes through the park. As soon as you walk around the corner from the car park, the noise and fumes of the traffic drop away, and the sense of space and quiet is amazing.

Walk 1: Walk to the first waymark on the right, turn left, and then follow the path as it leads away from the railway line (fenced) and into the peace and tranquillity of rural Kent.

Walk 2: Walk to the second waymark and select a trail to follow past the rape fields and into a secluded open valley beyond.

Facilities

Free car park. Campervan access.

M2 Junction 3

Syle Wood *ME5 9RJ*

Getting there

From Junction 3 take the A229 Maidstone, Chatham. At the Lord Lees roundabout take exit 3, A229 Chatham, Rochester. After half a mile turn left, signed Blue Bell Hill. Turn right, Common Road and park at The Robin Hood on the right.

Return to M2 Junction 3

Retrace the route to the A229, and turn left. At the roundabout take exit 4, signed London M2, to rejoin the motorway.

Walk

Return to the road and turn left. At a footpath sign walk left across a field. Stay on this path and head into the trees. After this, the path is a straight line heading gently downhill. Ignore all tracks to the left and right. Emerge from the wood and turn left onto a signed bridleway just before Upper Nathenden Farm. This path returns directly to The Robin Hood garden on a slight upward incline. Allow an hour for this 2.5 mile walk.

Facilities

At The Robin Hood (01634 861500). Pub food available 1200-1430. Big play area for children and an aviary with exotic birds.

Dogs are welcome in the bar and spacious garden seating area. A large dog water bowl is provided.

Campervan access.

ME7 3RG Capstone Farm Country Park

Getting there

From Junction 4 take the A278 signed Gillingham. At the next roundabout take exit 2, Rainham A278 and at the second roundabout take exit 2, Gillingham A2. Stay on the A2 over two more roundabouts. Turn left, signed Capstone Country Park. Go down the hill and take exit 1 at a mini-roundabout. At the second roundabout take exit 2, Capstone Farm Country Park. The car park is on the right.

Return to M2 Junction 4

Turn left from the car park and turn left (Almond Grove). Turn left again (Chapel Lane) and then right (Hempstead Valley Drive). At the roundabout, take exit 1 (Sharsted Way). At the next roundabout take exit 3 A278, signed London, Dover M2 to return to the motorway.

Walk

There are several paths and trails in this popular 280 acre park.

Join the main footpath, a track which runs parallel to the larger section of the car park. When this path goes slightly uphill, ignore a turning to the left and go straight on to walk through the Millennium Wood.

Then turn left at the far edge of Orchid Wood to skirt around Capstone Wood. Pass through Round Glade and return to the car park through the Millennium Wood.

Facilities

Free car park, closed at dusk. Café, WC+disabled, visitor centre 1000-1630 with maps, children's play area, pet centre. Campervan access.

Oad Street

ME9 8LB

Getting there

Leave the M2 at Junction 5 signed Sittingbourne, Channel Tunnel. At a roundabout take exit 4, A249 Maidstone. Turn left at a signpost to Bredgar, Tunstall (Pett Lane). Park at The Plough and Harrow or the craft centre car park.

Return to M2 Junction 5

Turn right out of the craft centre car park. At a T-junction turn left, signed Maidstone. At the next T-junction turn right. At the next junction turn left, signed M2/M20, to return to the motorway.

Walk

Turn right from the craft centre, or cross the road from The Plough and Harrow, and walk down the lane to a footpath sign on the left. Climb the stile and walk through a field with the hedge to the right, and a lovely view of a traditional oast house over to the left.

At the corner of the field follow the path round to the right and over another stile. Turn left and immediately right to walk between well-fenced horse paddocks. Go through the gate ahead and walk down towards the stables. Just after the stables keep a sharp eye out for a rickety stile to the left. Climb this stile and walk uphill to another stile. Turn right and walk with the fence on the right until the next (and final) stile. Walk straight on through a wooden kissing gate into a small rabbit-filled wood beyond.

Retrace this route to return.

Facilities

At The Plough and Harrow (01795 843351), open all day. Bar snacks and meals, log fire in winter. Well-behaved dogs on leads are welcome in the bar.

At craft centre: WC, tearoom, shop. Campervan access.

Perry Wood

Getting there
Leave the M2 at Junction 6 and take the A251 Ashford. Drive through North Street. Turn left, signed Selling, New House Lane. Stay on this lane, passing through Hogben's Hill, following signs to Selling. Drive through Selling, past Norham Farm on the left, and take the first right turn, signed Perry Wood and The Rose and Crown. At the crossroads turn left, signed Perry Wood car park, and the car park is on the left.

Return to M2 Junction 6
Turn right out of the car park and right again. At the T-junction turn left and drive through Selling. Continue through Hogben's Hill. Pass Newhouse Farm on the left and turn right, A251, at the crossroads. Continue on the A251 to rejoin the M2.

Walk
There are two information boards with walking information, and clearly signed paths through this enchanting wood.
Yellow arrows direct walkers on a short circular walk through an avenue of rhododendron and beech trees.
Perry Wood is a charming place to walk and think, with little trace of modern life.

Facilities
Free parking. The 18th century White Lion (01227 752211) in nearby Selling (ME13 9RQ) welcomes children and dogs. Bar/restaurant food available. Campervan access.

Dargate Wood *ME13 9HB*

Getting there

At Junction 7 continue on the A299. Branch left, signed Dargate. Turn left, High Street Road. Turn left, and then right onto Plum Pudding Lane and park at The Dove on the left.

Return to M2 Junction 7

Turn right from the car park, Plum Pudding Lane. After half a mile turn left. Take the next left and then merge onto the A299 to return to the M2 (London).

Walk

With The Dove behind you, walk to a Public Bridleway sign, just after Elm Tree Cottage.

Follow the path as it winds uphill into the woods, and when you look back there's a fabulous view of the Thames Estuary and the sea beyond.

The path is waymarked with blue posts, and is easy to follow. In Spring the wood is full of rabbits, squirrels and birdsong.

Turn round to return to The Dove at your own halfway time.

Facilities

The Dove (01227 751360) is a quaint Victorian country pub with marvellous food. Children are welcome. Dogs are allowed in the bar and garden area.

M3

From London to Southampton, via Bracknell and Winchester

Junction

M3 Junction 1

Northbound only

Hounslow Heath

Getting there

At Junction 1 continue forward on the A316 Central London. Branch left on the A314, Heathrow, Hounslow. Enter Hanworth. Turn left at the A312 (Uxbridge Road). At traffic lights, turn right, A244 Hounslow Road. Turn right to the A315, signed Hounslow. At the mini-roundabout by The Hussar pub turn right, and Hounslow Heath car park is on the right.

Return to M3 Junction 1

Turn left from the car park. Turn left by The Hussar, and continue straight at the traffic lights. At the traffic lights turn left, signed A244 Feltham. At the next traffic lights turn left. At the roundabout take exit 4 to return to the motorway.

Walk

Tamed as this large heath may appear today, it was once a haunt of highwaymen and women including the notorious Dick Turpin.

From the car park, go towards the information board to join a broad concrete track onto the heath and the start of the circular Crane Valley circular walk. This track probably dates from World War 1 when the heath was a base for London's aerial protection. Today it makes the heath accessible to wheelchair users. Continue through a field to a footpath sign, and the visitor centre facilities.

Facilities

Free parking 0800-dusk. WC+disabled, information centre. Campervan access.

Lightwater Country Park

Getting there

Leave the M3 at Junction 3 and take the A322 Guildford. At the roundabout get in the right hand lane for the A322 Guildford exit, and almost immediately take a sliproad to the right, signed Lightwater Country Park. Turn right at the tourist sign to Lightwater Country Park, The Avenue. The entrance to the park is at the end of the road.

Return to M3 Junction 3

Leave the park along The Avenue. Turn right at the T-junction on to the dual carriageway and at the roundabout rejoin the M3.

Walk

Circular trails of varying lengths start at the visitor centre, each featuring a different aspect of the park. The paths are surfaced, and fully accessible.
The Nature trail, marked with numbered posts, is a 40 minute walk.
The Heathland Trail is longer, with stunning views over the heathland. The Lakeside walk is the shortest, and gradient-free.
Maps of all the trails are available from the visitor centre.

Facilities

Free parking, open to dusk. WC+disabled. Children's play area. Refreshments at the leisure centre. Campervan access.

M3 Junction 4

Basingstoke Canal Centre *GU16 6DD*

Getting there

From Junction 4 take the A331 Guildford, Farnborough. Continue on the A331 until a branch to the left, signed Mytchett. The Basingstoke Canal Centre is well signed from here.

Return to M3 Junction 4

Turn right from the car park and straight over the mini-roundabout, Coleford Bridge Road. Turn left at a mini-roundabout, signed Farnborough Park. At the next roundabout, take exit 2 and merge with the A331 signed M3 to rejoin the motorway.

Walk

If it's flat walking you're after, then a towpath walk is ideal. Cross the bridge to the less crowded path, and turn left or right as the fancy takes you. The 32 mile towpath is a Site of Special Scientific Interest nature reserve, and a great place for spotting wildlife.

Facilities

Free parking 0930 to 2200. Café, WC, children's play area, picnic area, gift shop, visitor centre, canoe and pedalo hire, boat trips and a floating art gallery.

Getting there

From Junction 5 take the A287, Newnham. Park in The Hoggett car park, just before the traffic lights.

Return to M3 Junction 5

Turn left out of the car park onto the A287 and back to the motorway.

Walk

From the car park, cross to Holly Bush Lane. Walk past the immaculately kept mobile homes on the left and enter the common proper. The woodland path is quite narrow, but easy to follow as it winds through the old trees with their carpeting of bracken. There is only one small path so you won't get lost here. Walk until the trees begin to thin out and then bear left on the track to stay on the common.
Retrace your route to return to The Hoggett.

Facilities

At the Hoggett (01256 763009). Meals 1200-1400; 1830-2100. Friday breakfast 0700-0900. The imaginative menu features local produce. Dogs are welcome in the bar and at the outside tables. Campervan access.

M3 Junction 6

Basing Lime Pits

Getting there
From Junction 6, northbound take exit 1, southbound exit 2 at the roundabout. At the next roundabout take exit 3, Old Basing. Immediately turn left signed Basing Lime Pits (one-way). Park in either of the two car parks on the right, the first is better for children.

Return to M3 Junction 6
Turn right out of either car park. At the T-junction turn right, The Street, and then immediately turn right again, Brown Lane. At the traffic lights turn right, Park Lane. At the T-junction turn right, London Road. At the roundabout take exit 3 signed M3/London/South West to rejoin the motorway.

Walk
The two car parks are close together, and the walk starts from the top of the natural amphitheatre. Head uphill towards the left hand corner. There is a squeezer stile to the left of a dog bin which leads through onto common land beyond. This is a large, flat area which can be walked around in 25 minutes.

Facilities
Free parking. Children's play area and adventure playground by the first car park. Fitness trail. Campervan access.

The 16th century Crown Inn (01256 321424) is just a few moments away in Old Basing village. To save time you can phone your menu choices through in advance and have a meal waiting for you on arrival. Well-behaved dogs on leads are welcome in the bar and the outside garden area.

Getting there

From Junction 9 take the A272 Winchester, northbound exit 4, southbound exit 1. At the roundabout, take exit 1, A31 Alvesford, Alton. At the next roundabout follow signs to Easton, on Castle Lane. Enter Easton and continue to a T-junction. Park in The Cricketers' Inn car park.

Return to M3 Junction 9

Turn left from the car park and immediately right onto Castle Lane. At the roundabout take exit 2, signed M3. At the next roundabout take exit 2 signed M3 to rejoin the motorway.

Walk

From the car park, cross the road and follow signs for St Mary's church. Pass the lychgate and a look for the shell logo of the Pilgrim's Way, a long distance path from Winchester to Canterbury. Just after the Old Schoolhouse turn right, and then immediately left to a footpath sign. Cross the football pitch diagonally and through a kissing gate in a clump of trees in the corner.

Now follow the clear path with the River Itchen to the right, and keep going in this direction in a field – stile – field pattern until your half-way point. Turn round to return with the river to the left. Water loving dogs will adore this walk.

Facilities

At The Cricketers' Inn (01962 779 353). Home cooked food served between 1200-1400. Dogs are welcome in the public bar and outside tables. Dog water is provided. Campervan access.

St Catherine's Hill

Getting there
From Junction 10 take exit 1 at the roundabout signed St Catherine's P&R, Garnier Way. Drive over a small railway bridge and park in the car park immediately on the left before a river bridge.

Return to M3 Junction 10
Leave the car park and turn right. At the roundabout take exit 2. At the next roundabout take exit 2 signed M3 London, Basingstoke to return to the motorway.

Walk
Walk with the river on the right and keep walking for about 15 minutes until the path opens out, and you reach an information board at the entrance to St Catherine's Hill.
There's a long set of steps leading to the top and a splendid view of Winchester when you get there. The hill has been purposefully used for around 3000 years, with traces of Iron Age defenses, as well as a Norman chapel. It's a great place for a picnic on a sunny day.
This walk can also be continued alongside the river on a flat path if you want to skip the steps.
Turn round to return to the car park with the river on the left.

Facilities
Free car park. Campervan access.

SO21 2HW Otterbourne Park Wood

Getting there
From Junction 12 follow the sign to Chandlers Ford. At a mini-roundabout, take exit 2, Otterbourne Hill. Turn right onto Boyatt Lane, and left onto Park Lane and park.

Return to M3 Junction 12
Turn, and turn right at the end of Park Lane. At the T-junction turn right, Boyatt Lane. Pass The Otter on the left and turn left at the cross roads, Otterbourne Hill. At the roundabout take exit 1 to return to the M3.

Walk
Enter Otterbourne Park Wood on the signed footpath. This leads downhill on the outward leg of the walk, and uphill on the return section.
There are also many paths to the sides, and this is an enchanting place to ramble in at will.
Otterbourne Park Wood is a Heritage Site with gnarled ancient oak trees and traces of an old Roman road from Winchester.

Facilities
Free parking. Campervan access.
The Otter (0238 0252685) serves food, and is family and dog friendly.

M4

From London to South Wales, via Reading and Bristol

Junction

Getting there

Leave the M4 at Junction 3. At the roundabout take exit 1, Central London, A4. At the next roundabout take exit 2, A4 Central London. Pass Osterley Station on the left and look out for the tourist signs for Osterley Park.
Turn left just after the traffic lights and at the junction go straight on through the gates of Osterley Park.

Return to M4 Junction 3

Leave the park gates and go straight ahead to return to the traffic lights. Turn right onto the A4 to return to the M4.

Walk

With over 350 acres of sumptuous parkland to enjoy, this elegant walking space is a welcome contrast to the busy M4. There is one marked pathway within Osterley Park called the Nine Acre Path and this starts at the car park.
Equally pleasant is a wander past the lakes and to simply enjoy this luscious open space.
Dogs can run free in the north east meadow, signed from the car park.

Facilities

Car park 0800-1800, 1930 in summer, £3.50 National Trust members and disabled free. Free access to park. WC+disabled, tea room 1100-1700 with dogs at outside tables and shop. Charges apply to visit Robert Adam house and garden (NT) and dogs are not allowed. Farm shop with fresh fruit and veg.

Harmondsworth Moor *UB7 0AQ*

Getting there

From the Junction 4 exit roundabout take the A408 Uxbridge. Follow signs for 'All other routes'. Then quickly take the 1st left signed Harmondsworth. At the next roundabout take exit 2, A3044 Harmondsworth. Continue over a mini-roundabout and enter Harmondsworth. At the next mini-roundabout take exit 2, Harmondsworth High Street. Park in the free bays on the High Street.

Return to M4 Junction 4

Leave Harmondsworth on the High Street and take exit 2 at the mini-roundabout. At the next mini-roundabout take exit 2 signed M4. At the roundabout take exit 2 and return to the motorway as signed.

Walk

Start at Moor Lane to the left of the Five Bells and walk to a public footpath sign. Cross the bridge and turn right to enter an enclosed park, Harmondsworth Moor, which has benefitted from some creative park management.

Beyond the landscaped section and large adventure playground, stiles and gates lead into the surrounding rural woodland.

This is an enjoyable space for a short ramble, and a very convenient stopping point if you're waiting for a Heathrow arrival.

Facilities

At The Five Bells (0208 7594713) Pub fare served Mon-Sat, and Sunday carvery. Well-behaved dogs on leads are welcome in the front bar and at the outside tables front and rear. Campervan access.

Getting there

From Junction 7 take the A4, Maidenhead. Enter Burnham village. At the roundabout take exit 1, B3026 Eaton, Lake End Road. Enter Dorney and pass a pub on the right. Drive over the river and the car park is on the left.

Return to M4 Junction 7

Turn right from the car park. At the roundabout take exit 3 signed A4 Slough. At the next roundabout take exit 3 signed M4 and return to the motorway.

Walk

Walk to the clearly marked entrance to the Jubilee River Way. This is an all-access path along the side of the Jubilee 'River', actually a flood management device which has created 11km of wetlands.

Walk straight as far as the bridge where there is a choice of waymarked routes, as well as viewing platforms and information boards describing the wetlands. The public footpath running parallel to the main track divides walkers from cyclists. Turn round at your half way point to return to the car park.

Facilities

Free car park, with height restrictions. There's a Sainsburys on the Lake End Road roundabout for picnic supplies.

Chieveley Services *RG18 9XX*

Getting there
Leave the M4 at Junction 13 and follow signs to Chieveley Services/Costa. Park in the services car park as close to the Travelodge Motel as possible.

Return to M4 Junction 13
Turn left from the services and rejoin the motorway.

Walk
This is a truly rural walk, and a surprising contrast to the busy motorway and services nearby.
Walk past the Travelodge motel with the lorry and caravan parking area on the right, and between the wooden posts in the corner onto a lane. At the second footpath sign turn right to cross a stile into a field.
Go straight, with the service road to the right. At a red sign turn right and enter a field. Follow the yellow arrow to a lone tree some distance away.
At the tree, bear half left and follow the narrow path towards the trees ahead. Pass a group of three oak trees to reach a wooden footbridge over a brook. This brings you to a cart track, aptly named Marsh Lane.
Turn right and walk as far as the farm before turning round. In hot weather, this is a fantastic place to cool overheated travelling dogs, with plenty of drinking water and splashing opportunities in the brook.
Retrace your steps to return to the car park.

Facilities
Moto motorway services with Costa, M&S, Burger King. Children's play area. Campervan access.

Getting there

From Junction 15, take the A419 Swindon. Take the 1st left, A4259 Swindon. At the roundabout take exit 1, A4259 Swindon. At the next roundabout take exit 1, signed Coate Water to reach the car park down a lane on the left.

Return to M4 Junction 15

Leave the car park and at the roundabout take exit 5, signed M4. Pass a Texaco petrol station on the left, and get in lane to return to the M4 at the next roundabout.

Walk

This is a fine all-weather walk on a hard surface path around the lake.
From the car park walk up the incline to the information board. The signed path around Coate Water is 4 miles of flat, easy walking. As this is a circular walk, it's easy to walk as little or as long as you want and turn around at a time that suits you.

Facilities

Free car park, WC, café, picnic area, BBQ area, children's play area, ranger on duty.
The Sun Inn (01793 523292) is adjacent to the lake, and a popular stop for families with children. Pub food available 1200-1430. Dogs are welcome in the large beer garden.

Lydiard Park SN5 3PA

Getting there
From Junction 16 take the A3102 Swindon. At the next roundabout take exit 1, West Swindon, Lydiard Park. At the next roundabout take exit 1, Lydiard Park and Hook. Turn right signed Lydiard Park and turn left into the car park.

Return to M4 Junction 16
Turn right from the car park and then left onto the main road.

At the roundabout take exit 3, M4, Wootton Bassett.

At the next roundabout take exit 3, M4.

Walk
Pass the visitor centre and café and turn right at a wooden post for the circular Lakeside Walk. Walk straight ahead with the side of Lydiard House to the left, to follow the rolling grassland gently downhill to the lake. Cross the bridge on the left and then turn right into a wooded area. Pass some picnic tables and follow the path round to return to the green.

There is plenty of space to relax and ramble in this 260 acre park, and non-walkers may enjoy a visit to the house and museum.

Facilities
Car park free, closes at dusk, WC+disabled, café, visitor centre, children's playground and exhibitions. Campervan access.

Lydiard House and Walled Gardens open Tues-Sun 1100-1700. Entrance charges apply.

SN14 6JB Kington St Michael

Getting there
From Junction 17 take the A429 Cirencester. Turn left, signed Grittleton, Stanton St Quinton. Enter Stanton St Quinton and turn left, signed Kington St Michael, Kington Lane.
Enter Kington St Michael, turn left at the T-junction and park at The Jolly Huntsman on the right.
There is more parking space opposite the village hall a little further on for non-patrons.

Return to M4 Junction 17
Turn right from the car park. Turn left at the crossroads. Turn left onto the A350. Continue on the A350 to return to the M4.

Walk
Turn left from the car park, walk past the Almshouses on the left and turn right at a Public Bridleway sign.
When the path divides, by a metal gate, take the right hand path to walk through a meadow. In the summer this is a mass of wildflowers and the path is fringed with sweetly-scented chamomile.
Follow the clear path as far as the cottage on the left, and then turn around to return.

Facilities
At The Jolly Huntsman (01249 750305). Lunch 1200-1400. Well-behaved dogs on leads are welcome inside. Campervan access.

M4 Junction 24

Caerleon *NP18 1QQ*

Getting there

From Junction 24 take the B4237 signed Newport. Turn right onto the B236 Caerleon, Royal Oak Hill. Turn right, signed The Bell Inn. Park in The Bell Inn car park on the right.

Return to M4 Junction 24

Turn left from the car park and left again up the hill. Continue to a T-junction and turn left, unsigned. This road returns directly to the M4.

Walk

Turn right from the car park to walk down the quiet lane beyond the pub for a few minutes until a public footpath sign on the right by a wooden gate, just after a house called Ty Bryn.

The path begins with some steps up a steepish bank, with a metal fence to the right. As the ground levels it opens out and on a clear day there's a magnificent view over the River Usk and the town of Caerleon below.

Continue to follow the clear signs for the Usk Valley Way walk, with a blue and white otter symbol, and turn round at your own halfway point and return to The Bell.

Facilities

The Bell (01633 420613) A traditional inn open 1100-2300 serving locally-sourced food. Well-behaved dogs on leads welcome in the front bar area.

Campervan access.

Caerleon has claims to be the ancient town of Camelot. The modern town is built around an earlier Roman garrison, and the Roman amphitheatre is open to visitors.

NP10 9GN Monmouth and Brecon Canal

Getting there

From Junction 27 take the B4591 signed High Cross, eastbound exit 1, westbound exit 3. Turn right, Cefn Walk, signed Fourteen Lock Canal Centre. The canal centre car park is on the right, just over a canal bridge.

Return to M4 Junction 27

Turn left out of the car park, over the canal bridge, and at the T-junction turn left. Follow this road to rejoin the motorway.

Walk

Walk away from the visitor centre, to a gravel path leading downhill, passing top-up ponds for the canal system. When the path divides into steep and steeper, choose the steep one and walk through the vestiges of the fourteen locks, where the engineering skills of the Victorians can't fail to impress.

The 'steeper' path follows the route of the canal through woodland and, if you don't mind the stiff climb back to the car park, is the longer walk of the two.

Facilities

Free car park, locked at dusk. WC, Visitor Centre (01633 894 802) closed Tues and Wed. Campervan access.

Small mini-market by the canal bridge for simple picnic fare.

M4 Junction 28

Tredegar House *NP10 8YW*

Getting there

From Junction 28 take exit 4 eastbound, exit 2 westbound signed Tredegar House. Follow the sliproad to the left, signed A48 and Tredegar House. At the lights turn left, and exit 1 at the roundabout to enter the grounds of Tredegar House.

Return to M4 Junction 28

Exit the grounds and take exit 4 at the roundabout to join the A48 Newport. At the traffic lights turn right, signed M4/A48 Newport, and follow the A48 to return to the motorway.

Walk

Go through the visitor centre entrance and continue round to the front of Tredegar House to enter the 90 acre parkland and Woodland Trail. Dogs can run off-lead here.

This is an ideal walk if you're travelling with non-walkers as there's so much to see in and around the house.

Tredegar House was once home to the notorious Morgan family of pirates.

The House has been a TV location for Dracula, Dr Who and Torchwood.

Facilities

Car park, charge £1.80. WC+disabled, café, craft shops, free dog poo bags from the visitor centre. Campervan access.
Also formal gardens and 17th century house.

Coed Coesau Whips

Getting there

From the Junction 30 roundabout take the turning for Rudry. At a mini-roundabout take exit 2, signed Through Traffic. This is a narrow lane with passing places. Pass a farm on the right and then turn left at a T-junction, signed Lisvane, and a Forestry Commission car park is on the right.

Return to M4 Junctlon 32

Turn left out of the car park and take the first right turn, unsigned. At the mini-roundabout continue straight to rejoin the motorway.

Walk

Take the broad track leading gently uphill between the trees. In wet weather this track is the firmest path and provides a clear route to follow.

It's uphill for the first half and then downhill on the way back. There are also enticing trails off to the left and right which are worth exploring.

This is a dream spot for dog walkers, and a delightfully remote place to ramble in glorious solitude.

Facilities

Free parking at forest. Campervan access.

Cardiff Gate motorway services are on the exit roundabout from the motorway.

Castell Coch

Getting there
From Junction 32 take the A4054 Tongwynglais. Enter Tongwynglais and turn right at The Lewis Arms, signed Castell Coch.
Turn left at the Castell Coch tourist sign and drive up the hill to the car park.

Return to M4 Junction 32
Leave the castle grounds through the narrow gateway and turn right. Turn left at the T-junction and continue to rejoin the M4.

Walk
Before starting this walk, it's worth taking a free look at this fairytale castle from the path around the base.
Castell Coch has been a location for Doctor Who, and was Cackle's Academy in The Worst Witch TV series.
The walk starts from the top car park by the castle entrance. Turn up the hill on a clear path under the trees near an information board, and join the waymarked Taff Trail.
The Trail runs from the castle to the town of Caerphilly, with the opportunity for a walk as long and as strenuous as you wish.

Facilities
Free car park 0930-1830. Campervan access.
WC, café and shop inside the castle. Castle entrance £3.60 adults, £10.00 family ticket. Guide dogs permitted inside.

Getting there

From Junction 33 take the A4232 Cardiff, Penarth, Barry. Take the first slip road off the dual carriageway signed Museum of Welsh Life.

Return to M4 Junction 33

Exit the car park to the A4232 and return to the M4.

Walk

A museum may seem a strange place for a walk, but this a 100 acre museum. As part of the experience you walk outdoors peeping in at traditional Welsh dwellings, or shopping at a working bakery with superb fresh bread and cakes for sale. There's also a school, farm, chapel and craft workshops.

Dogs are welcome in the museum, but may enjoy a dog walk before going in. Look for the yellow public footpath sign behind the car park security lodge, and join the path to walk with the river to the left. This is a 'there and back' walk, so turn round when you're ready.

Facilities

Car park £3.00, includes museum admission, 1000-1700. WC+disabled, café, shops, exhibits. Hard surface paths. Campervan access.

Free dog poo bags from reception. Dog water bowls.

M4 Junction 34

Tyn-y-Coed Forest

Getting there

From Junction 34 take the A4119, eastbound exit 1, westbound exit 3. At the traffic lights turn right, signed Groes Faen. After Groes Faen turn right, Tynant Road. Enter Creigiau and turn left at the T-junction. Turn right, Tyn-y-Coed Road. A small Forestry Commission car park is on the left, shortly after a hospital driveway.

Return to M4 Junction 34

Turn right out of the car park. At the cross roads turn left. Pass a golf club and turn right, Tynant Road. At the T-junction turn right, Groes Faen, with the Dynevor Arms on the left. At the next T-junction turn left, signed M4.

Walk

Walk down the shingle track leading from the car park and through a kissing gate (wheelchair accessible) to enter the forest. A route is waymarked, although there is essentially just one surfaced, all-weather path here.
With no navigational skills necessary, this is a great place to inhale big lungfuls of healthy forest air.

Facilities

Free parking at Tyn-y-Coed. Campervan access.
At The Dynevor Arms (0292 0890530, CF72 8NS) pub food served 1200-1400; 1800-2100. Dogs on leads are welcome in the bar and garden.

Getting there

Follow signs to Bryncethin. Enter Bryncethin, Bryncoch and turn left at a roundabout. At a T-junction turn left.
At the next roundabout turn right, signed Abergwr A4065. Enter Brynmenin and turn right, signed Bryngarw. Turn right, signed Bryngarw, to enter the grounds of Bryngarw House, and the car park is on the right.

Return to M4 Junction 36

Leave the car park and grounds to turn left at the T-junction. Turn left again at the next T-junction and continue straight on the A4065 Bridgend. At the roundabout, take the 2nd exit, signed M4 and A4061 Bridgend. At the lights turn right, signed M4, and return to the motorway.

Walk

Walk past the house towards the plant nursery. Turn right at the unmarked public footpath just before the nursery gate. After a few paces there is a yellow waymark arrow. Follow these yellow markers and ignore all other trail signs.
Pass a pond on the right and to another yellow waymark. Go over a stile and into the ocean of bracken beyond. The path opens out to give a stunning vista of the valleys and ridge beyond. Follow the path into the woodland ahead, and retrace the route to return.

Facilities

At Bryngarw: Free parking in term time. WC+disabled, information room, garden centre. Café/snacks available during school holidays. Campervan access.
Sarn Park motorway services are at the M4 exit.

Kenfig Dunes CF33 4PT

Getting there

From Junction 37 take the A4229 Porthcawl. At the next two roundabouts take the A4229 Porthcawl. Then immediately turn right signed Kenfig. Pass a holiday park on the right, and turn right at a T-junction. Enter Kenfig and park in a small car park on the left by a nature centre.

Return to M4 Junction 37

Turn right out of the car park. Turn left after the golf clubhouse. Pass the holiday park and turn left at the T-junction, signed Port Talbot M4.
At the roundabout take exit 1, M4 to return to the motorway.

Walk

The walk starts at the yellow waymark arrow behind the nature reserve building. Take a sandy track into the dunes to a green waymark arrow. Follow the green arrows for a circular sweep through the dunes. Look out for the rare Fen Orchid as you walk through carpets of wildflowers and exotic reed beds.
Kenfig has plenty of drama, from sunken villages to ghosts. It is an outstandingly attractive area, and has been featured in the TV 'Coast' series.

Facilities

Free parking. WC and information at the nature centre, 1400-1630 weekdays, 1000-1630 weekends. Campervan access.
The Prince of Wales (01656 740356) just beyond the car park is a popular local pub, and dogs are welcome in the bar.

Afon Argoed Forest

Getting there
From Junction 40 take the A4107 Cymer. At the roundabout turn left, Cymer, Afon Argoed Forest. Continue for nearly 6 miles until the Afon Forest Park and visitor centre is signed to the right.

Return to M4 Junction 40
Turn left from the car park to the A4107, signed Port Talbot. At the mini-roundabout turn right, signed M4 and Port Talbot, and rejoin the motorway.

Walk
Afon Forest is a vast 11,000 hectares and a centre for outdoor pursuits, including mountain biking, bird watching, and hiking.
There are six marked trails of varying lengths, all starting at the visitor centre. This is unbeatable walking country, and it's worth allowing plenty of time for extreme leg stretching. Walkers and mountain bikes are kept apart by some very skilled route planning, so stay safely on the trails.

Facilities
Car park £1.50. WC, visitor centre, café, shop, dog water bowls, mountain bike hire. Campervan access.

Cwm Clydach

Getting there

From Junction 45 take the A4067(N) signed Pontadawe. At the roundabout take exit 1, B4291 Clydach. At a mini-roundabout go straight (B4603) and then take exit 2 at the next mini-roundabout. Leave the town and continue. Pass The New Inn on the right, cross a river bridge and take an immediate right turn to enter the Cwm Clydach car park.

Return to M4 Junction 45

Turn left from the car park and continue. Take exit 1 at a mini-roundabout, A4067 Swansea. At the next roundabout take exit 3, A4067 Swansea, M4.

Walk

Walk through the metal gate to enter the nature reserve. There is just one path here, which runs alongside the River Clydach, so the route is there-and-back. The path itself is exceptionally well maintained, and stays firm in wet weather.

Facilities

Free parking in nature reserve car park. Campervan access. At The New Inn (01792 842839). Pub food 1200-1430. Children's play area. Dogs are allowed in the beer and rear gardens.

Getting there

From Junction 46 follow signs to Felindre. Enter Felindre. Turn right, signed Ammanford, Brynammon. Turn right again at a no through road sign and park at The Shepherds Country Inn.

Return to M4 Junction 46

Turn left from the car park and left at the T-junction. Turn left at the next T-junction, and continue to the M4.

Walk

Turn right to walk up a lane past a trout fishery. Turn right at a green footpath sign. Cross a stile with waymark for the Gower Way.

Bear half right across a field and over another stile. Turn left and walk through an avenue of big bracken. Cross two wooden footbridges to follow the path along the side of a valley. Climb the next two stiles and continue as waymarked over a series of wooden walkways above boggy ground.

Rounding a corner, the outer wall of the Lliw reservoir is visible ahead. Climb one final stile to reach a metal lane at the corner of the reservoir and then turn right to reach the visitor centre and cafe. Reverse the route to return.

Facilities

At the Shepherds Country Inn (01792 794715). Bar meals, children's playground. Dogs on leads welcome in the bar and beer garden.

At the Lliw reservoir. WC, outdoor café, dog water.

M5

From Birmingham to Exeter,
via Worcester and Bristol

Junction

B32 3DS Woodgate Valley Country Park

Getting there

From Junction 3 take the A456 Kidderminster. Enter Halesowen and take the first left (unsigned), Lapal Lane South. Turn left just before a no through road sign. At a crossroads turn right and then take exit 1 from the roundabout signed South Woodgate. The entrance to Woodgate Valley Country Park is on the left.

Return to M5 Junction 3

Turn right out of the park and return to the A456, and turn left. Continue to the roundabout at the bottom of the hill and double back to return to the motorway.

Walk

Three marked trails between one and three miles have been created through the park, and maps are supplied at the visitor centre. Off-trail walking is encouraged within the 450 acres of the valley.

This is gentle, green rolling countryside and it is hard to imagine that the heart of Birmingham is pumping not so very far away.

Facilities

Free parking. Park closes 1900 summer, 1630 winter. WC, refreshments, visitor centre with outdoor seating, picnic area, children's play area. Campervan access.

M5 Junction 4

Waseley Hills

Getting there

From Junction 4 take the A491 Stourbridge. Turn right signed Waseley Hills Country Park, B4551, Money Lane. Opposite a pub turn right, signed Waseley Hills Country Park. Turn right into the park and visitor centre.

Return to M5 Junction 4

Turn left from the park and continue to a T-junction and turn left B4551. At the junction with the A491 turn left to rejoin the M5.

Walk

There are two clearly marked walks over the Waseley Hills. Both trails start at the visitor centre and handy descriptive leaflets can be picked up before you start.

The Fox Trail (90 minutes) makes a circuit of the whole park and is clearly signed with orange markers.

The shorter Badger Trail (30-40 minutes and purple markers) gives magnificent views of the Black Country and Worcestershire on a bright day.

Facilities

P&D car park, 1 hour 50p Mon-Fri, weekends and bank holidays £1.00, disabled badge holders free. Open sunrise to sunset.

WC+disabled, visitor centre, café, children's play area. Campervan access.

Piper's Hill

Getting there

From Junction 5 follow signs to Bromsgrove A38. Enter Wychbold and take the second right, Chequers Lane. At a T-junction turn left, Stoke Lane. Turn right, Astwood Lane.
At the T-junction by The Country Girl turn right, Hanbury Road and turn right to a car park just before a bend to the right.

Return to M5 Junction 5

Turn left from the car park. Turn left after The Country Girl. At the T-junction to Shore Lane turn left, Wychbold, and follow signs to return to the motorway.

Walk

Follow the path into the trees and downhill. Pass a large pond to the left and continue past Knotts Farm on the right to enter woodland.
Continue ahead on a clear path through glades of majestic trees. At a waymark post go straight on. Join a track, and follow the waymarked route ahead. Continue into a field through a kissing gate.
Follow the clearly marked footpath to the church and then retrace your steps through the wood and past Knotts Farm to return to the car park.

Facilities

Free car park. Campervan access.
At the Country Girl (01527 821790; B60 4AY) Open 1200-2300, lunch served 1200-1430. Children welcome. Well behaved dogs allowed outside. Dog water provided.

Worcester Woods *WR5 2LG*

Getting there

From Junction 7 take the A44 Worcester, Evesham. Continue on the A44 over two roundabouts and at the next roundabout take the A4440 Evesham. At the next roundabout take exit 1, signed Country Park and enter Worcester Woods.

Return to M5 Junction 7

Leave the car park take exit 3 at the roundabout, signed M5. Take exit 1 at the next roundabout and then rejoin the motorway.

Walk

Bear to the left of the visitor centre to a wooden sign for the woodland trail. Walk up the track and turn left at a waymark to the start of two 30 minute stile-free trails: a Woodland Trail, and a Meadows Trail.
Paths are well maintained and provide easy walking around this fully accessible route. Apparently, present day Nunnery Wood was once cultivated by Cistercian nuns, who must have been pretty brawny to win a living from this land.

Facilities

Free parking. WC+disabled, visitor centre, café, picnic area, BBQ area, shop, children's playground. Campervan access.

Getting there

From Junction 11A follow signs to reach the A417 Cirencester. Crickley Hill Country Park is signed from the A417 Stow on the Wold roundabout onwards. The car parks are at the end of the entry lane.

Return to M5 Junction 11A

Leave the car park and turn right at the end of the lane.
At the T-junction turn right, signed A417 Cirencester. Stay in the right hand lane to take exit 2 A5/A417 signed Cheltenham Central and then follow signs to rejoin the M5.

Walk

There are marked routes for five walks of varying lengths, with descriptions and colour codes displayed on an information board. All walks start at the visitor centre. At the start of the trails there's a viewpoint, with the Malvern Hills, Gloucester Cathedral and the Black Mountains visible on a clear day.
The Family Trail (orange) is 0.5 miles, has no stiles, and is fairly buggy-friendly.
There are three 40 minute / 0.75 mile walks: Hill Fort Trail, Scrubs Trail and the Scarpe Trail. The Park Trail is slightly longer. All the trails are easy to follow, the main difference between them being the amount of shade in summer, or mud in wet weather.

Facilities

Free parking. WC, visitor centre (April-Sept), picnic area, free dog poo bags in car park, dog water bowls.

M5 Junction 13

Frampton Green *GL2 7DY*

Getting there

From Junction 13 take the A419/A38 Dursley. Turn right, B4071 Frampton on Severn. Enter Frampton and turn left, signed Frampton Green and churches. Look for The Three Horseshoes on the right, and park nearby.

Return to M5 Junction 13

Return to the T-junction and turn right, signed Gloucester. At the next T-junction turn left, A38 Gloucester/M5. At the roundabout take exit 2, signed A419 Stroud/M5 and rejoin the motorway at the next roundabout.

Walk

Cross the road from The Three Horseshoes to walk past Rosamunde House, and round a metal gate to the left of the sailing club entrance. Take the left hand path at the footpath sign ahead. Climb two stiles (there's a dog gate on the second stile) and head across a field, aiming for a brushwood arch. Climb a stile to the left of the arch and bear half-left and through a gate ahead. Cross the lane after the next gate, passing a house called Fitcherberry East, and through another gate. Aim for the weeping willows by the lake beyond. Turn at the lake to return to the village green.

Facilities

At the Three Horseshoes (01452 740463). This is what village pubs are all about! Well-behaved dogs are welcome in the bar, food and snacks are available, and strangers are greeted with lively interest. Campervan access.

Getting there
From Junction 17 take the B4055, Easter Compton. Continue to Easter Compton and park at The Fox Inn on the left.

Return to M5 Junction 17
Turn right from the Fox Inn car park and return to the motorway, B4055.

Walk
Cross the road from The Fox and turn left. Turn right at a white gate marked 'Collingwood' and cross the stile ahead. Follow a footpath arrow across the first field, and climb a stile to enter field 2. Walk across the field diagonally, with an electric pole to the left.

Go through a gate to field 3 and follow the arrow into field 4 and walk diagonally to the far right hand corner. Climb two stiles and enter field 5. Walk along the left side of the field with the fence on the left. Turn round here for a 30 minute walk.

Facilities
At The Fox Inn. Food and snacks served. Well behaved dogs on leads are welcome in the bar, dog water provided. Campervan access.

Enthusiasts will love the skittle alley here.

M5 Junction 18

Northbound only

Blaise Castle Estate

Getting there

Leave the M5 at Junction 18 to take the A4 signed Bristol, Docks. Remain on the A4 Bristol until a left turn, B4054 Shirehampton. Turn left, B4057 for the signed public car park on the right.

Return to M5 Junction 18

Turn left out of the car park. At the traffic lights turn right (Sylvan Way). Turn right at the next traffic lights, signed M5. At the roundabout take exit 2 signed M5 and watch carefully for the lane changes.

Walk

This is an enormous outdoor space, with a mixture of woodlands, meadows and limestone gorge spread over 650 acres.

Signed trails lead from the car park in all directions across the land, to the point that you're spoiled for choice. Many paths are hard-surfaced for buggy and wheelchair accessibility.

The dog-friendliness of the estate is obvious as soon as you walk towards the café, and are greeted by a large contemporary dog sculpture, with built-in water bowl.

On sunny public holidays this is a popular destination and you may find queues for the café and car park.

Facilities

Free car park, café, WC+disabled, dog water provided at café entrance, children's play area. Campervan access.

Leigh Woods

Getting there

From Junction 19 take the A369 Easton in Gordano. Proceed on the A369. Pass The George in Abbots Leigh and turn left at the slightly obscured sign to Leigh Woods. Continue up a long driveway to reach the car park on the left.

Return to M5 Junction 19

Turn right out of the entrance lane, A369, and continue to return the M5.

Walk

This is a fabulous walk through Forestry Commission woods with clear paths and easy to follow routes.

Two marked trails start from the car park. The red route is two miles. The purple route is a little shorter at 1.5 miles and passes by the site of an iron-age hill fort.

It is also easy to ramble through the trees picking your own route underneath the canopy of trees. When we were here the birdsong was awesome and the wood was as close to deserted as anyone could wish.

Facilities

Free parking to 2100. Campervan access.

Sand Point

Getting there

From Junction 21 take the A370 Weston-super-Mare. Take the first exit off the A370, signed B3440 Kewstoke. At the traffic lights turn right, Kewstoke. Pass a McDonalds on the left and follow signs to Kewstoke over several small roundabouts. Enter Kewstoke and continue straight. Turn right signed Sand Bay. Turn right at the T-junction, Sand Point Only, and park at the end of the lane.

Return to M5 Junction 21

Turn left out of the car park, and left again into Sand Road, signed Bristol. At the T-junction turn left, signed Worle.
Continue over the next three roundabouts. Get into the left hand lane before the T-junction and follow signs to rejoin the M5.

Walk

Enter the Middle Hope Nature reserve on the surfaced path to the right of the information board. The circular path is easy to follow, and keen eyes may spot the site of a motte and bailey castle, the remains of Thomas a Becket's Priory, or even a Neolithic barrow.
Dog walkers may prefer the beach walk. The beach is large, and there is also a path parallel to the lane which stretches for miles.

Facilities

Free parking, campervan access. WC. National Trust dog toilet area, dog water bowls.
Tearoom with home-baked cakes on Sand Road.

BS24 0JL Sedgemoor Services

Getting there
Sedgemoor Services are between M5 Junctions 22 and 21 on the northbound side of the motorway. No southbound access.

Return to M5 northbound
As signed from Sedgemoor Services.

Walk
Park on the left side of the car park. Walk past a No Entry sign to a service road and over a cattle grid. Turn left and pass Strowland Cottage. Turn right at a footpath sign and follow a yellow pointer across a field and cross a wooden footbridge and stile hidden in the hedge. Brent Knoll is on the left.
Walk with the hedge to the right and the Knoll ahead. Keep a pylon on the left and cross a footbridge into the third field. Turn round here for a 30 minute walk.
Brent Knoll was once an island. Folk lore says it was created from a wayward shovelful of soil thrown here by the same giant who dug out the Cheddar Gorge.

Facilities
RoadChef motorway services. Costa, Eat-in, Wimpy. Picnic area. Children's playground. Days Inn motel (dog friendly). Campervan access.

Mark River Walk TA9 4LT

Getting there
From Junction 22 take exit 1, A38 Highbridge. Take the first left, B3139 Mark. At a T-junction turn left, B3139 Mark. Enter Mark, and park at The White Horse Inn on the left.

Return to M5 Junction 22
Turn right from the car park and follow the lane back through Mark. Turn right signed A38/M5 Edith Meade. Turn right at the T-junction, A38 Bristol. At the roundabout take exit 3 and rejoin the motorway.

Walk
Walk left from the car park, passing in front of The White Horse. Continue past some cottages with Vole Road to the left to a Public Bridleway.
This becomes a grassy track with water flowing on the right. The path is some 2.5m wide with plenty of dog romping space and an abundance of wildlife.
Follow the water for as far as you wish and turn round to return to The White Horse.

Facilities
At the White Horse Inn (01278 641234). Food available Mon-Fri 1130-1500; 1730-2100. Sat-Sun 1200-2100. Beer garden, children's play area. Dogs welcome in the bar and beer garden. Campervan access.

TA7 8PN Bawdrip, Somerset Levels

Getting there
From Junction 23 take the A39 Glastonbury/Wells. At a T-junction turn left, A39 Glastonbury. After 300 yards turn left to The Knowle Inn car park.

Return to M5 Junction 23
Turn left from the car park and turn right onto the A39 to return to the motorway.

Walk
Cross the road in front of the pub and turn right. Immediately turn left at a footpath sign. This soon becomes a secluded path between two high hedges. After the left side hedge stops, climb a stile on the right to walk across the field and over the next stile.

Follow the yellow arrow to the left in field 2. Walk with the hedge to the left around the corner of the field to a gate on the left. Cross the next stile by the gate and continue to a footbridge and one more stile.

Cross King Sedgmoor's Drain bridge and turn right after the kissing gate to walk with the water on the right. For a 35 minute walk, turn round here.

The walk can be extended by continuing along the waterside.

Facilities
At the 16th century Knowle Inn (01278 683330). Quality meals and snacks served all day, and cream teas. Garden chipmunk tree for children. Well-behaved dogs on leads are welcome in the large beer garden and public bar. Campervan access.

Maunsel Lower Lock

Getting there

From Junction 24 take the A38 Bridgwater, Minehead. At the next roundabout take exit 1, Taunton A38. Enter North Petherton and turn left after a church, signed North Newton. At North Newton turn left (Maunsel Road) and follow the small tourist signs for 'Canalside Walk'. Eventually turn left, signed Canal Centre/Bankland. The car park is on the left before the canal bridge.

Return to M5 Junction 24

Turn right from the car park. At the T-junction turn right and follow the brown signs to Maunsel House. Enter North Newton. Continue to a T-junction and turn right, signed Bridgwater. At the next T-junction turn right, A38 Bridgwater. At a small roundabout take exit 3 to return to the M5.

Walk

Cross the canal bridge and walk down to the canal. The towing path to the right is hard surfaced, wide, and suitable for all weathers and shoes. The path in the opposite direction is unsurfaced, muddier, and more popular with dog walkers.

Facilities

Free parking, WC, Tea Rooms (Wed-Sun 1030-1700).
Bridgwater Moto motorway services at the M5 exit roundabout with Burgerking, Eat Fresh and WH Smith. Campervan access.

Getting there

From Junction 26 take the Blackmore/Ruggin turn. At a T-junction turn right, signed Ford Street. Bear right as the road forks, and at a T-junction turn left, signed Ford Street. Continue through Ford Street, ignoring all side turnings. At the top of the hill turn left, signed Kingsmeade Centre and continue to park at The Merry Harriers on the right.

Return to M5 Junction 26

Turn left from the car park. At the crossroads turn right, signed Wellington. Continue through Ford Street and then turn right, signed Blackmore. At the next signpost turn left, signed Wellington, to return to the M5.

Walk

Cross the road and bear right. Turn left at a Public Bridleway sign on the left. Go through a gate, and follow the arrow straight ahead. There is a splendid view over the countryside below from this point. Follow the track downhill through the trees and then turn round and return uphill to The Merry Harriers.

Facilities

At the Merry Harriers (01823 421270), a gastro pub with award-winning food. Open Tuesday evening to Sunday afternoon. Well behaved, clean dogs are permitted in the bar and large outdoor area.

Campervan access.

M5 Junction 27

Sampford Peverell *EX16 7BJ*

Getting there

From Junction 27 take the A361 Barnstaple/Tiverton. Take the 1st slip road, left, and at a mini-roundabout turn left, signed Sampford Peverell. Enter Sampford Peverell and park at The Globe Inn on the right.

Return to M5 Junction 27

Turn left from the car park, continue to the roundabout and take exit 3. Rejoin the M5 at the next roundabout.

Walk

Walk to the rear of the overspill car park and up the small flight of steps leading straight onto the towing path of the Grand Western Canal.

This canal was intended to link the Bristol and English channels, but that 19th century grand plan was never completed and now the 11 miles or so of canal has become the Great Western Canal country park.

Look out for horse-drawn barges hauling their burden of 21st century tourists along the towing path.

Facilities

At the timbered Globe Inn (01884 821214). All day opening and food. Children's playground with lots of activities. Dogs welcome in the public bar and outside.

Campervan parking on-road if the entry archway to the car park is a challenge.

Haldon Forest

Getting there

Leave the M5 and follow the A380 Torquay. After a long bend to the right, turn left signed Great Howelden. Pass a café and turn left at a give way sign. Turn right, signed Ashcombe/Dawlish. At a crossroads go straight, signed Ashcombe. Turn left into the Mamhead Forest car park.

Return to M5 Junction 31

Turn right from the car park. At the crossroads turn left, signed Chudleigh/Newton Abbot. At the dual carriageway turn left A380 Torquay. Turn onto the B3192, Teignmouth. At the roundabout take exit 3 signed Exeter M5. Pass a Texaco garage on the left, merge with the A38 and continue forward following signs to the M5.

Walk

There is a circular trail around Haldon Forest that starts at the information board in the car park. The path is fully accessible and marked with a blue shoeprint symbol. On a clear day you can see Exmouth, the Black Forest and the Jurassic coastline.

An ideal spot for a picnic and some quiet time at the furthest point of the M5.

Facilities

Free parking. Picnic area. Campervan access.

M6

From Rugby to Carlisle, via Birmingham and Preston

Junction

Swift Valley Nature Reserve

Getting there

From Junction 1 take the A426 Rugby, northbound exit 1, southbound exit 3. At the roundabout take exit 2, Rugby A426. At the next roundabout take exit 3, Brownsover Hall. The entrance to the nature reserve car park is on the right after the Brownsover Hall Hotel.

Return to M6 Junction 1

Leave the car park and turn immediately right at the top of the slope, and then left onto the main road, signed M6, M1. Follow signs at three successive roundabouts to return to the motorway.

Walk

Follow the path slightly uphill from the car park to reach a canal bridge and go through a gate into the field beyond.
Walk across the lower part of the field to the next gate, which leads onto a tranquil towpath by a disused canal that's now a haven for wildlife.
At a blue footpath sign turn away from the towpath into wilder woodland territory. This path is clearly signed and returns directly to the car park.

Facilities

Free parking, 2.1m height restriction. Free dog poo bag dispenser in car park.
Non-residents welcome at the adjacent Brownsover Hall Hotel (0844 855 9123). Dogs may accompany owners to the elegant outside seating area.

Oxford Canal *CV7 9HZ*

Getting there
From Junction 2 take the B4065, signed Ansty. Enter Ansty, and park at The Rose and Castle Inn on the right.

Return to M6 Junction 2
Turn left from the car park, and return to the M6 on the B4065.

Walk
The 77 mile Oxford canal links Oxford with Coventry. Unlike other industrial canal routes, the Oxford canal never became a 19th century cargo super-highway and so today it has become one of the most enjoyable rural towpath walks in the country.
From the rear of the car park walk down to the canal. Cross the bridge and through a gate on the right to reach the towpath. Turn right and walk under the bridge.
A walk to Bridge 19 and back is a 30 minute stroll, with the option to make a longer walk by simply continuing along the towpath.

Facilities
At the Rose and Castle (024 7661 2822). Food served all day. Dogs allowed in rear outdoor seating area. Campervan access.

Getting there

From Junction 3 take the B4113, Bedworth. At the next roundabout take exit 2, Bedworth B4113. At the traffic lights turn right, Black Horse Road. At a mini roundabout take exit 2. Cross a canal bridge and turn left to park by The Greyhound.

Return to M6 Junction 3

Leave The Greyhound and turn right. Continue on Black Horse Road to a T-junction. Turn left, B4113. At the roundabout take exit 3, signed M6, and return to the motorway.

Walk

The Canal Art Trail towpath walk between Hawkesbury Junction and the Coventry Basin is interesting and different as it features artworks commissioned from local artists.

Look out for the imposing statue of the famous 18th century canal engineer James Brindley in particular.

The path is well-maintained and buggy-friendly.

The complete Art Trail is 5 miles, and leads into the City of Coventry.

Facilities

At the traditional canalside Greyhound Inn (02476 363046). Well-behaved dogs are welcome in the bar area here, and children are permitted inside until 1900. Campervan access.

Sutton Park *B74 2YT*

Getting there

From Junction 7 take the A34, Birmingham. At the second set of traffic lights turn left, Queslett Road. At a roundabout go straight, Brownhills A4041. At the next roundabout turn right, King's Road. At the next roundabout take exit 3, Rough Road. Continue until a left turn signed Tamworth A453. Pass a leisure centre and turn left to enter Sutton Park.

Return to M6 Junction 7

Leave through the Town Gate and turn right. At the traffic lights turn right, Monmouth Drive. Go straight at the lights and take exit 3 at the roundabout, King's Road. At the next roundabout turn left. Continue straight at the next roundabout and turn right at the lights, A34 to return to the M6.

Walk

Sutton Park is the largest urban park in Europe with 2,400 acres of open space containing seven lakes and a mixed terrain of heathland, woodlands, wetlands and marshes. Stop at the visitor centre to pick up a leaflet of the eight varied walk routes here. Archaeological walk routes trace a Roman road, and evidence of prehistoric Brummies. You may see wild cattle and ponies, or even a stoat on one of the nature trails.

Facilities

P&D car parks 0900 to dusk. WC+disabled, visitor centre. Café, bistro, steakhouse within the park. Rangers on duty throughout the park. Free dog poo bags from visitor centre. Campervan access.

Shoal Hill

Getting there

Leave the M6 at Junction 12 and take the A5 Cannock. Turn left, Huntington, opposite the Four Crosses pub. At a cross roads, go straight signed Huntington, Cocksparrow Lane. Shoal Hill car park is the first turning on the right.

Return to M6 Junction 12

Turn left from the car park. At the cross roads go straight across. Continue and turn right onto the A5 to return to the M6.

Walk

This is a magnificent walk over the lower reach of Cannock Chase. The land is laced with paths and the open heathland means it is easy to navigate. There are no signed trails.
The paths leading away from the car park incline gently upward, and so to return to the car park you head gently downward.

Facilities

Free car park (closes at dusk), with height restriction.
At the 17th century Four Crosses Inn (01543 503309, WS11 1RX)

M6 Junction 13

Acton Trussell *ST17 0RJ*

Getting there
From Junction 13 take the A449 Stafford. At a roundabout take exit 3 signed Acton Trussell (Mill Lane). Enter Acton Trussell and continue to the Moat House and car park at the far end of the village.

Return to M6 Junction 13
Turn left out of the car park and continue through the village. Turn left at the roundabout, A449 Wolverhampton and M6, and rejoin the motorway.

Walk
Walk past the entrance to the Moat House. Go through a gate and turn left. Turn left again following a yellow footpath sign over the canal bridge.
Turn left onto the towing path of the Staffordshire and Worcestershire canal and enjoy a flat but interesting walk past brightly painted narrowboats and calm Staffordshire countryside.
The path is well maintained and delightfully rural.

Facilities
At the 14th century Moat House (01785 712217). Food available all day.
Dogs are welcome at the outdoor tables by the side of the lake. Dog water is provided.
Campervan access.

Getting there

From Junction 14 take the A5013 Eccleshall. Pass through Creswell and Gt Bridgford and turn right at a tourist sign for The Mill at Worston, Worston Lane. Park at The Mill on the left.

Return to M6 Junction 14

Turn right from the car park. At the T-junction turn left, and continue to return to the M6.

Walk

Return to the road and turn right past a livery stable. Cross to a footpath sign and follow a yellow marker down a track. Follow the track on the left into a field, and walk through to the next yellow waymark and over a stile, with dog hole. Cross a brook to enter the next field and follow the track straight on. Turn round at the gate at the end of this field to return the same way.

Facilities

At The Mill (01785 282710). Food available 1100-2100, children's play area, easy wheelchair access. Dogs welcome in garden only. Inside the 13th century Mill is a fascinating display of milling artefacts and ruralia. Campervan access.

Hanchurch Hills

Getting there

From Junction 15 take the A519, Eccleshall, Shrewsbury. Enter Hanchurch. At the traffic lights continue on the A519 and turn right, signed Stableford. Continue until the start of woodland, and turn left to the car parks.

Return to M6 Junction 15

Turn right out of the car park, and then left at the end of the lane to the A519. Stay on the A519 to rejoin the M6.

Walk

There are several clearly marked trails in these wonderful woods, and the trail markers start from the second car park. The Red route is about 2 miles (40 minutes), and the Green trail is just over 3 miles (90 minutes). If you have the time, there's a Blue trail at 7 miles.

The woodland here is perfect for children and dogs to really let off steam. Even on the hottest of days, the cooling canopy of branches provides shade.

Facilities

Free car park. Picnic tables. Campervan access.

Getting there
From Junction 16 take the B5078 Alsager. Turn left, signed Barthomley and park by The White Lion Inn in the village.

Return to M6 Junction 16
Leave the village and turn right at a T-junction onto the B5078 to return to the M6.

Walk
From the White Lion go to the church and turn left at a footpath sign. Pass the rectory and walk with a hedge to the right. Climb a stile with dog gate, bear left and over the next stile to enter a large field. Walk with the hedgerow to the left and cross the field with a dewpond to the left.
At the hedge at the far side, turn right to hunt for the almost invisible stile in the far corner. Carry straight across the next field, aiming for a metal gate and stile near the trees. Follow the arrow over the stile to a gate and waymark ahead. Turn round here for a 40 minute walk.

Facilities
At the White Lion Inn (01270 882242). This 16th century inn seems to be the second home of the entire village. Food served. Dogs on leads are welcome inside, with own water bowl if possible.

Brereton Heath

Getting there
From Junction 18 take the A54 Holmes Chapel. Enter Holmes Chapel and continue, signed Congleton. Turn right, Davenport Lane, and the entrance to Brereton Heath Nature Reserve is on the left.

Return to M6 Junction 18
Turn right out of the car park. Turn left onto the A54 and continue to rejoin the motorway.

Walk
There are a number of trails in this 50 acre nature reserve, including an easy access trail around the perimeter of the lake.
Trail leaflets can be picked up from the information centre, and rangers are on hand to give advice.
Dog owners are encouraged to explore the woodland trails surrounding the lake, which is a popular dog swimming venue.

Facilities
Car park 70p/one hour, open 0830 to dusk. Visitor centre, WC+disabled, picnic tables. Campervan access.

Spud Wood

Getting there

From Junction 20 follow signs to join the B5158 Lymm. Enter Lymm and turn right signed A56 Altrincham. At a roundabout turn left, Oughtrington Lane. Turn right after a canal bridge, Stage Lane. Spud Wood car park is on the right, unsigned.

Return to M6 Junction 20

Turn left out of the car park and then left onto Oughtrington Crescent. At the T-junction turn right, Higher Lane. Then turn left onto Elm Tree Road and continue to the M6.

Walk

This is a fabulous walking spot, with several good walks.
A canal walk gives the choice of a 1.5 mile walk to the pretty town of Lymm, or a 2.5 mile walk to Dunham Park in the other direction.
The Timberland Trail starts at the car park. Cross the canal bridge and follow the signed path into Spud Wood, newly planted by the Woodland Trust.
A wheelchair accessible path is marked, and the path is flat with a light gravel surface.

Facilities

Free parking. Campervan access. Shops and cafes in nearby Lymm, and a petrol station on the way with WCs and a small shop.

Culcheth Linear Park *WA3 4AB*

Getting there

From Junction 22 take exit 1 southbound, exit 3 northbound, Winwick Lane. Turn right at a sign to Croft, Sandy Brow Lane. At a T-junction in Croft turn left, Mustard Lane. The entrance to Culcheth Linear Park is a sharp turn to the left after a bridge.

Return to M6 Junction 22

Turn right out of the car park. Turn right after the school in Croft, signed Lowton. Turn left at the T-junction to return to the M6.

Walk

The park is linear because it used to be a railway line to Wigan. Now though, it's a dreamy countryside environment in the Mersey Forest with hardly anyone around except walkers.

The park is about 2 miles long, with a circular route for a 45 minute walk. Free walks leaflets are available at the ranger cabin. The main path is hard surfaced and suitable for wheelchair users and buggies.

Facilities

Free parking, picnic tables, ranger cabin. Campervan access. At The Cherry Tree, Culcheth (01925 762624; WA3 4EX). A modern pub serving food 1100-2130. Dogs are welcome in the outdoor seating areas.

Getting there

From Junction 23 take the A580 Manchester. Turn left, signed Pennington Flash, A579, Bolton. Then turn left at traffic lights and turn right into Pennington Flash when signed, opposite a fire station.

Return to M6 Junction 23

Turn left out of the park and turn right at the traffic lights signed M6/Manchester A579. At the next traffic lights turn right, signed M6/A580 and continue to return to the M6.

Walk

There's plenty of space here for a good long walk, either on the signed trails or just rambling around the 200 hectares of the park.

The main feature is the huge lake or 'flash', which is home to a host of wildfowl including some black swans.

To reach the trails, pass the children's play area and then there is a choice of a water path by the lake or a woodland path.

The paths are well maintained and fully accessible, but shared with cyclists and horses.

Facilities

P&D car park, blue badge holders free. WC+disabled, information centre, mobile café, children's play area, dog water bowls. Campervan access.

Beacon Country Park *WN8 7RU*

Getting there

From Junction 26 follow signs to reach the A577 Wigan and continue for 2 miles. Turn right onto Mill Lane and continue to Beacon Country Park. There are two car parks, the second is nearer to the visitor centre and facilities.

Return to M6 Junction 26

Turn right from both car parks. Turn left onto the A577 and follow signs to return to the M6.

Walk

There are well signed paths leading out from both car parks. The terrain is a mixture of woodland and open grassland, with enough space for a good 45 minute walk or longer.
To reach the facilities at the visitor centre, leave either car park and follow the direction indicated on the trails. Wheelchair users can join an accessible circular track from the visitor centre, or from the second car park.

Facilities

Free parking, WC+disabled, visitor centre, café, dog water, ranger office. Campervan access.

Cuerden Valley Park

Getting there

Leave the M6 at Junction 28 and turn right, signed A49 Euxton. Follow the brown signs to Cuerden Valley Park, going straight on at the traffic lights on Lancaster Lane. Go straight on at a mini-roundabout, leave the residential area and the Wigan Road car park is signed on the left.

Return to M6 Junction 28

Leave the Wigan Road car park and turn right. At the mini-roundabout continue straight and rejoin the M6 as signed.

Walk

With 650 acres there is plenty of good walking at Cuerden Valley Park, and the marked paths are just a starting point. Take the gravel multi-access path from the car park and continue to a signed footpath to the lake. Turn right on the other side of the lake and follow the path through Dog Kennel Wood and Gravel Hole Wood. Turn right onto the multi-user path and then left, signed visitor centre. Walk past the front of Cuerden Hall to the Cinder Path. Turn left on the multi-user path to return to the car park.

Facilities

Five free car parks (6ft 6 height restriction). WC+disabled. Visitor centre, vending machine drinks. Picnic supplies available at Sainsburys, off the A6/A49 junction.

Scorton Nature Trail *PR3 1BY*

Getting there

From Junction 33 take the A6, Garstang, Blackpool. Turn left at the staggered junction, Whinney Brow Lane. At a T-junction turn right, and then left over a railway. Turn right, Richmond Hill Lane. At JC Country Shop turn left, Clevely Park Lane. Turn left at the sign for Scorton Picnic Site car park.

Return to M6 Junction 33

Turn right from the car park, and then turn right at Miller's Brow. Turn left, Richmond Hill Lane. Turn left and then right after the railway bridge. Turn left, Whinney Brow Lane. Turn right at the A6 junction with the A6. Take exit 2 at the roundabout to rejoin the M6.

Walk

This is a hugely enjoyable 30-40 minute circular woodland walk with one well signed path making navigation easy.
Start from the rear left corner of the car park on a well maintained track. Continue, following the circular walk route marked with white arrows.
A shallow river on the left at the start of the walk is ideal for cooling down journey-cooked dogs.

Facilities

Picnic tables at the start of the walk.
At JC Country Shop and Café (01524 791362). WC+disabled, cafe, farm shop, outdoor clothing and pet supplies. Campervan access.

Crook o'Lune

Getting there

From Junction 34 take the A683 Kirkby Lonsdale. Turn left, Dennydeck Lane, unsigned just before a group of cottages. Cross the 6ft wide bridge and turn right at a crossroads, Low Road. Turn left at a tourist sign to Crook o' Lune picnic site. Parking for wider vehicles and wheelchair users is just before the narrow bridge.

Return to M6 Junction 34

Turn right from the car park and turn left, Station Road just before The Greyhound Inn. Breathe in and cross the bridge again. Turn right at the T-junction to return to the M6.

Walk

Paths within the Lune Millennium Park roughly follow the River Lune from Glasson to Lancaster and Bull Beck near Caton. Start at the Station 6 car park and go downhill on the single path to the river valley below. It's a 45 minute, 2km, walk to Bull Beck, where there's a picnic area and WC.
The riverside path, starting at the alternative car park before the narrow bridge is gradient-free and hard-surfaced. Pass the old station to join the Bull Beck path.

Facilities

Station 6: free parking to dusk. WC+radar, café, walk info.
At Bull Beck: WC+disabled, picnic tables. Campervan access.

M6 Junction 38

Tebay Village *CA10 3UY*

Getting there

From Junction 38 take the A685 Kendal. Park at The Cross Keys Inn on the right or on the lane by the churchyard.

Return to M6 Junction 38

Turn left from the car park and at the roundabout take exit 1 to rejoin the motorway.

Walk

Turn left out of the car park and left again, this is Church Street. Walk downhill with the churchyard to the left to find a yellow waymark arrow, and then follow more yellow arrows leading around a barn.

Turn left onto a track and go straight on at a bridleway sign. Cross the river bridge ahead.

Turn right at a footpath sign to walk with the river on the right and pass underneath the motorway. Then continue on the path and over two stiles into a large field.

Towards the end of this field the remains of a motte and bailey castle can be reached by stepping stones. The river is broad, clean and shallow here.

For a 40 minute walk, this is a good place to turn round.

Facilities

At the Cross Keys (0153 9624240). Dogs are welcome in the bar, and water is available. Campervan access.

CA10 2NN Pooley Bridge, Ullswater

Getting there

From Junction 40 take the A66 Keswick. At a roundabout take exit 2, A592 Ullswater. Turn left, B5320 Pooley Bridge. Park in the Dunmallard car park before the bridge.

Return to M6 Junction 40

Turn right from the car park. Turn right when signed, A592 M6/Penrith. At the roundabout take exit 2 to return to the motorway.

Walk

The walk starts at the rear of the car park, where the path is very clear. Walk through the woodland with the clean and shallow River Eamont to the right, and eventually emerge into a field. Continue to walk along the river bank for just under a mile, and then turn round to return to the car park.

Facilities

P&D parking, Blue Badge holders free. Campervan access.

At the timbered Pooley Bridge Inn (017684 86215) home cooked food served 1200-2030. Well-behaved dogs welcome throughout.

Outdoor gear shops, gift shops and steamer trips on Ullswater.

Wetheral CA4 8ES

Getting there
From Junction 42 take the B6263 Wetheral. Drive through Cumwhinton and enter Wetheral. Pass the village green on the right, and turn right by the general store. Park at The Crown Hotel on the left, non-patrons on the lane.

Return to M6 Junction 42
Turn left at the T-junction by the General Stores. Continue on this road to return to the M6.

Walk
There's a lot to admire on this walk, which combines a fabulous riverscape and fine walking with samples of glorious architectural bling.

Walk downhill from the hotel, past the station and down a flight of 99 steps. Turn right onto a lane, past a church, and then turn left to reach the River Eden.

Don't miss the stone bench with faux-Victorian cushioned seats here, created by sculptor Tom Shutter.

Turn right and continue on the riverside path until a point opposite a waterfall on the other side of the river. Go up the steps and into Wetheral Woods, a slumbering ancient wood. After enjoying the wood for a while, turn around to return.

To avoid climbing up the 99 steps, take the grassy slope to cut through the churchyard, turn right on the lane, and then right by the village stores.

Facilities
At the Walton's Bar in the Crown Hotel (01228 561888). Good selection of meals 1200-1400 and snacks. Well behaved dogs on leads are welcome in the large bar area. Campervan access.

Getting there

From Junction 44 (and A74) take the A689, Hexham and exit 1 at the next roundabout, A689. Turn right, signed Low Crosby. Enter Low Crosby and park in The Stag Inn car park.

Return to M6 Junction 44

Turn right out of the car park and right at the T-junction, Carlisle A689. At the roundabout take exit 3 signed M6/Scotland.

Walk

This is a flat, green and lovely walk along the river to Linstock and back.

From the car park, turn right onto the road and follow the signed footpath for the Hadrian's Wall Path.

Walk to the end of the short lane and turn left, ignoring the first footpath sign and stile.

Then turn right to walk with the River Eden on the left, in the direction of Linstock on the Hadrian's Wall path, full of atmosphere and a sense of history even though none of the wall remains.

Facilities

At the Stag Inn (01228 573210). Lunch served 1200-1400 Tues-Sun in summer. Dogs are welcome in the beer garden. Campervan access.

M11

From London to Cambridge, via Harlow

Junction

CM16 6PU Epping Long Green

Getting there

From Junction 7 take the B1393, Epping. Pass a McDonalds on the left. Enter Thornwood Common and turn right signed Epping Green, Uplands Road. Park in The Travellers Friend car park.

Return to M11 Junction 7

Turn right from The Travellers Friend. At the crossroads, turn left, B1393. Continue to return to the M11.

Walk

Leave the car park and turn right down a broad grassy track, Epping Long Green. The path along this linear village green is 2.5km in total. Early one Sunday morning in spring, this track was sparkling with dewy May bloom and buttercups with no trace of the 21st century to be seen or heard. A delight for dogs and drivers.

Facilities

At the The Travellers Friend. (01992 572462) Open 1100-2300. Well behaved dogs are welcome in the bar. Campervan access.

Hatfield Forest

Getting there

From Junction 8 take the B1256, Takeley. Enter Takeley and turn right opposite The Green Man, signed Hatfield Forest. Turn right where signed to enter the forest and car parks.

Return to M11 Junction 8

Turn left at the forest exit, and left again onto the B1256 to return to the M11 interchange.

Walk

There are a number of planned trails, including a discovery trail for children within this enormous forest and a leaflet of routes can be bought from the NT kiosk on entry.
If you're just here for a short stroll, then it's easy to find a convenient pathway from your starting point for a ramble through the trees.

Facilities

National Trust car park charge £4.50, NT members free. WC+disabled, café, shop. All-terrain pushchairs for loan.
Dogs that may chase wildlife must be kept on leads, other dogs off-lead except by the lake. Campervan access.
Birchhanger Green Services (Welcome Break) at the M11 exit.

Getting there
From Junction 10 take the A505 Royston. Turn right signed Thriplow, Gravel Pit Lane. At a crossroads turn left, Farm Lane. Bear right onto Lower Street and the Green Man (painted blue) is on the left.

Return to M11 Junction 10
Turn right from The Green Man car park and bear left, Farm Lane. Turn right at the crossroads and then turn left at the A505 to rejoin the motorway at the next roundabout.

Walk
Turn right from The Green Man and then turn left at a footpath sign by Yew Tree Cottage. At the end, turn left onto a lane and immediately right at the next footpath sign. Follow the footpath signs to walk over fields to Church Lane. Turn right at a metal swing-gate and pass Bacon's Farm. Turn left at a Bridleway sign. Walk for 20 minutes or so along this broad track passing an RSPB information board describing the birds found in this area and then retrace the route to the Green Man.

Facilities
The Green Man (01763 208855) serves light lunches and specials, using fresh local produce. Well-behaved dogs on leads are welcome in the rear garden. Campervan access.
The Imperial War Museum and the American Air Museum at Duxford are nearby attractions.

Grantchester Meadows *CB3 9NF*

Getting there

From Junction 12 take the A603 Cambridge at the roundabout and then merge onto the Grantchester road. At the T-junction turn right, Coton Road, enter Grantchester and then turn left to reach The Red Lion car park. There's additional parking at the village charity car park on the right at the end of the village. This is a huge field, close to Byron's Pool.

Return to M11 Junction 12

Turn right onto High Street. Turn left, Coton Road. At the roundabout take exit 1, A603 and continue to return to the M11.

Walk

Turn right from the car park to enter Grantchester Meadows. There are two paths here, the higher path is hard surfaced and used by buggies, bikes and wheelchairs. The lower path hugs the river, and there are many access slopes to the river for dog swimming. Both paths are easy to follow, and can be combined to form a 40 minute circular route.

Facilities

At The Red Lion (01223 840121). Food served 1100-2100. Children's play area. ATM machine. Dogs on leads are welcome at the outside tables. Campervan access.
Village charity car park - £2.00 in honesty box.

M18

From Rotherham to Goole, via Doncaster

Junction

Roche Abbey

Getting there

From Junction 1 take the A631 towards Maltby, following tourist signs to Roche Abbey. Turn right where signed, down a steep cobbled private road with parking for Abbey visitors at the bottom.

Return to M18 Junction 1

Ascend the cobbled track, turn left. At the T-junction turn left onto the A631 and return to the M18.

Walk

This is a circular walk around the perimeter of the abbey ruins.

Walk through the abbey entrance and continue to the green footpath signs. Turn right, marked 'Doorstep' walk. Keep the ruins to the right and climb over a stile to cross the fast-running stream and past a small waterfall. Follow the path over some stepping stones. Then walk with the lake on the left and follow the winding path back to the car park.

An access path is marked on the information board. This seems to run from the entry gate, past the ruins, and into the grassy land beyond. In wet weather the ground could be soft.

Facilities

Free parking 0600-1830. WC+disabled when the Abbey (English Heritage) is open.

DN2 6BB — Sandall Beat Woods

Getting there

From Junction 4 take the A18, Doncaster and Doncaster Racecourse. Follow signs to the racecourse and turn left into Gate 8 from Leger Way. Continue to the car park at the end of the lane.

Return to M18 Junction 4

Turn right from Gate 8 and take the A18, Thorpe at the next three roundabouts. At the next roundabout, take exit 3, A630 Scunthorpe. Continue to return to the M18.

Walk

Sandall Beat Wood is much bigger than it seems, with dozens of criss-crossing paths encouraging walkers to explore the woods.
Follow the main track from the car park, and turn left to the visitor centre and facilities. There's a sturdy play area for kids here, with lots to climb and slide on.
The wood continues beyond the playground, either over a footbridge or by heading away from the visitor centre on one of the many paths.

Facilities

Free car park. WC. Access paths. Children's play area.

Waterside *DN8 4JQ*

Getting there
From Junction 6 turn into Waterside Road, northbound exit 1, southbound exit 4, a no through road. Bear left to park in the John Bull Inn car park or in the roadside parking bays.

Return to M18 Junction 6
Leave the village along Waterside Road and rejoin the motorway at the roundabout.

Walk
Walk past the front of the pub and continue along the short lane. At the last house take a track to the right of a post and then turn right at a stile and footpath sign. Walk with the water to the right on a pleasant grassy track, crossing a couple more stiles. All the stiles have spaces for dogs to get round or under.

At the end of the watery ditch walk up the bank on the right and turn right on a raised path along the side of a large flood plain. Stay on this path until the end of the village and a 5-bar gate. Go over the stile and turn right onto a track and back to The John Bull.

Facilities
At The John Bull Inn (01405 814677). Pub food served 1200-1400. Thomas Crapper was born in Waterside and adverts for his early water closet designs adorn the walls. Well-behaved dogs are welcome in the bar, dog water provided. Campervan access.

M20

From London to Folkestone, via Ashford

Junction

M20 Junction 2

Trosley Country Park *DA13 0SG*

Getting there

From Junction 2 follow signs to the A227, Meopham and Wrotham. Turn right off the A227 signed Trosley Country Park. Turn right, Waterlow Road, signed Trosley Park and Tea Rooms. After 60m turn right into the park entrance.

Return to M20 Junction 2

Turn left out of the park, and then left again at Waterlow Road.

Turn left, A227, and return to the M20.

Walk

Three walks of varying lengths and terrain are marked with colour coded posts. The red walk is flat, and takes around 60 mins. The blue walk is hilly and steep in places. The yellow walk offers easy access.

Trosley Park was formerly part of the Trosley Towers Estate, and is 160 acres of woodland and chalk downland. Look out for rare plants and animals here, such as the musk orchid and the chalkhill blue butterfly.

Facilities

P&D car parks £1.00. WC+disabled, refreshments, maps and information board, dog warden on duty. Free dog poo bag dispenser. Campervan access.

Manor Park Country Park

Getting there
From Junction 4 follow signs to West Malling, Rochester. At a roundabout take exit 1, A228 Tonbridge. At the traffic lights turn right, A20, signed West Malling. At a roundabout turn left, West Malling. Go through the town centre and the signed entrance to Manor Park is on the left.

Return to M20 Junction 4
Turn right from the park and through West Malling town centre. At the roundabout take exit 2, A20 Maidstone. At the traffic lights turn left, A228 Rochester. Turn left, A228, and join the M20 at the next roundabout.

Walk
There is one marked footpath, through copses of trees, wide grassy areas and a lake in this spacious aristo-park, once part of an 18th century estate created by Thomas Douce. Look out for the rare breed cattle that graze here and as it is a nature conservation site you may get to spot some less familiar birds and plants too.

Facilities
P&D car park £1.00; £1.50 weekends, closes dusk. WC+disabled, small café, children's play area. Map and information board. Campervan access.
Shops for picnic supplies in West Malling.

Thurnham *ME14 3LD*

Getting there
From Junction 7 follow signs to Maidstone. At a roundabout take exit 1, Bearsted, and exit 1 at the next roundabout. Turn left, Hockers Lane, and enter Detling. At a Post Office turn right, Thurnham. At Thurnham park at The Black Horse Inn, non-patrons with permission from reception.

Return to M20 Junction 7
Turn left out of the car park and drive to Detling. At the centre of the village turn left, The Street. Drive over the motorway and turn right at a crossroads. Take exit 2 at two roundabouts to rejoin the M20.

Walk
Turn left, Thurnham Lane, and walk uphill. Turn left at a stile on the left, White Horse Wood. Take a diagonal route downhill to cross a stile and turn right to a wooden kissing gate on the right. Turn left down the hill and cross over lane (Pilgrims' Way) into the field ahead, a pole marks the spot. Follow the path diagonally to the left to a church. Walk through the churchyard and turn left at the lane and back to The Black Horse.

Facilities
At the 18th century Black Horse Inn (01622 739170). Open all day. Reservations advised for evening meals. Outside shaded seating. Well-behaved dogs on leads welcome. Campervan access.

Getting there

From Junction 9 follow the A251 Faversham. Keep straight at the next four roundabouts, A251, and turn left at the traffic lights, A251 Faversham. Continue for 3.5 miles and take a sharp right turn into the King's Wood Car Park.

Return to M20 Junction 9

Turn left towards Ashford A251. After 3.5 miles turn right at the traffic lights signed M20, Ashford. Take exit 2 at the next three roundabouts, and exit 3 at the next roundabout and return to the M20.

Walk

Footpaths are clearly marked throughout the 1,500 acres of the wood with a choice of routes between one and five miles.

For the 3 mile 'Beech Walk' take the signed path to the left of the picnic area to follow the meandering paths through the ancient forest, and enjoy the leafy views across the valleys.

This was once a royal hunting forest and herds of deer still remain. You are more likely to see sculptures than deer though, as this is the main site of the Stour Valley Arts Project.

Facilities

Free parking. Information board with routes. Campervan access.

M25

London Orbital

Junction

Farningham Woods Nature Reserve

Getting there

From Junction 3 take the A20, West Kingsdown. Continue at the next roundabout, A20. At the next roundabout take the A225, Dartford. Drive under the motorway and turn left on Calfstock Lane, single track. The car park is at the end of the lane.

Return to M25 Junction 3

Return along Calfstock Lane and turn right, A225.
At two successive roundabouts take exit 3, A20 Swanley and rejoin the M25.

Walk

This is a quiet and atmospheric woodland walk in a nature reserve that is a haven of meditative calm.
An easy to follow 1.6 mile circular walk is marked, and the paths are clear and well maintained. On entering the wood there is virtually no sign of human existence. Lovely.

Facilities

Free parking at woods. Campervan access.
In Farningham village: The Lion Hotel (01322 860621; DA4 0DP). Country pub serving food 1200-2130. Dogs welcome in large garden, water bowls provided.

Marden Park

Getting there

From Junction 6 take the A22 East Grinstead. At a roundabout take exit 1, Oxted, Westerham A25. Take the first left, Tandridge Hill Lane. Continue as the lane becomes single track. At a T-junction, turn left and a small off-road parking area is immediately to the right.

Return to M25 Junction 6

Return down Tandridge Hill Lane. Turn right at the T-junction, A25. Take exit 3, London, at the roundabout, and continue to the M25.

Walk

The North Downs Way runs through Marden Wood but for a shorter stroll, take any path from the parking area leading downhill through the woods to a lush grassy meadow.
The paths here are easy to follow, and the birdsong and wildlife rustlings in this unspoiled wood are a delight.
Marden Park was once owned by the orchestral conductor Sir Adrian Boult and is now managed and maintained by the Woodland Trust.

Facilities

None at Marden Park.
The Nags End garden centre on the A20 has a café and WC.

Getting there
From Junction 8 take the A217, London, Sutton. Continue on the A217 over a roundabout and turn left signed Mogador, Stubbs Lane. At a crossroads continue, signed Mogador and Banstead Heath. Bear right and park in the rear car park at The Sportsman.

Return to M25 Junction 8
Reverse the route to the A217 and turn left. Proceed to a roundabout, approx 0.5 miles to U-turn and return to the motorway from the A217.

Walk
There are waymarked paths across the Heath, and the area is popular with riders and walkers alike.
Banstead Heath is part of the extensive Banstead Downs, and forms part of the green 'lung' around London. There is a mixture of open heath and woodland, and generally flat walking. There is so much space that the Heath is a delight to ramble around.

Facilities
At The Sportsman (01737 246655) a gastro-pub serving meals and snacks. Dogs welcome inside and out, dog water provided. Campervan access.
Several petrol stations on both sides of the A217.

Ashtead Common KT22 0DP

Getting there
From Junction 9 take the A243, London.
Pass the Leatherhead Golf Club and park at The Star on the left.

Return to M25 Junction 9
Turn right onto the A243 and return to the M25.

Walk
Ashtead Common is an enormous 500 acres and will easily satisfy the most energetic of walkers.
Cross the A243 at the refuge. Bear right and turn left at a Public Right of Way sign to Ashtead Common. A circular route through the woodland is marked on an information board at the entrance. The footpaths start through brushwood entries and lead through glades of old oaks and abundant greenery.

Facilities
At The Star (01372 842416). Meals and snacks served 1200-2200. Free Wi-Fi, children's activities. Dogs permitted in the bar and beer garden. Water bowls are provided. Campervan access.

Ockham Common

Getting there

From Junction 10 take the A3 Guildford, Portsmouth. Get into the left hand lane, and turn left immediately after a pedestrian bridge, signed Ockham Common. Enter the car park on the left.

Return to M25 Junction 10

Return to the A3, turning left onto the dual carriageway. Proceed until the first slip road exit and make a U-turn at the roundabout to return to the A3 (London) and M25.

Walk

Ockham Common is a site of special scientific interest as well as a favourite destination for families and dog walkers. Forest maps and walking routes are available at the refreshment kiosk in the car park.

Dog walkers will appreciate the Link Path from the car park to Boldermere Lake, crossing the road to walk over meadows to the lake. Fishing is forbidden at the lake, so water loving dogs can splash without restraint.

Facilities

Free parking to 1800. WC+disabled, refreshment kiosk, maps. Campervan access.

Runnymede *TW20 0AE*

Getting there
From Junction 13 take the A30 Egham. Stay in the left lane (A30) and loop under the motorway. At the next roundabout take exit 3, A308 Windsor. Turn right, signed Pleasure Grounds, to enter the car park.

Return to M25 Junction 13
Turn left out of the car park. At the roundabout take exit 1 signed M25 to return to the motorway.

Walk
This is a large, bucolic city green with much to offer. On a warm summer's day expect to see families enjoying their picnics underneath gazebos and tents, and children are well catered for with a brightly painted old-fashioned merry-go-round and bouncy castle.
From the car park, head towards the river to join the Thames Path national trail. This is part of a trail that runs alongside the Thames from its source to the sea.

Facilities
P&D parking. WC+disabled, café, children's playground and funfair. River boat trips. Campervan access.

WD3 5LW — Chorleywood Common

Getting there
Leave the M25 at Junction 18 and take the A404 signed Chorleywood and Amersham. Shortly after the signed turning to a cemetery on the right, turn left into the unsigned car park on the left.

Return to M25 Junction 18
Leave the car park and turn right. Continue to rejoin the M25.

Walk
There's excellent walking on this ancient common, with plenty of space for the travel-weary dog to spread his paws and fly into the bracken.

Follow the path from the car park and wander at will in the grassy spaces and woodland on the clear paths.

Now part of the Chilterns Area of Outstanding Beauty, the Common was mentioned in the Domesday Book.

Facilities
Free car park, with height restrictions.

At the nearby Rose & Crown Inn (01923 283841). Lunch served Tues-Sun, closed Mondays. Well behaved dogs are welcome in the bar and beer garden, dog water is provided.

Waterside walk *WD4 8RE*

Getting there
From Junction 20 take the A41, London NW and Watford. At the traffic lights turn left, signed Abbots Langley. The Waterside is on the left just after a canal bridge.

Return to M25 Junction 20
Turn left from the Waterside car park. Turn right at the traffic lights, signed A41 Hemel Hempstead and follow this road to return to the M25.

Walk
Turn left from the car park to cross the canal bridge, and access the towing path down the steep paths on either side of the bridge.
Turn left at a yellow footpath arrow to walk in the direction of Birmingham. This is the Grand Union Canal Walk. Pass a winding hole, where the sight of a narrow boat turning round can entertain, and continue as the path becomes more and more rural. Turn around at your half-way point to return to The Waterside.

Facilities
At The Waterside (01923 262307). Italian menu, food served 1200-1500, 1800-2100. Children's play area. Dogs welcome in the large garden, and outdoor covered area. Dog water provided. Campervan access.

EN6 3QQ South Mimms Services

Getting there
Follow signs to South Mimms Services and park by the Day's Inn Motel.

Return to M25 Junction 23
Follow signs to the M25.

Walk
A path between the motel and services building leads to the Wash Lane Common nature reserve. Turn left and walk to a metal gate and go into a field at a Public Bridleway sign. Turn right, with the hedge on the right, and walk around two sides of the field. Ignore a right turn and continue on the footpath. Climb a stile ahead and walk through the next field. Turn round here for a 30 minute walk.

Facilities
Welcome Break motorway facilities. Burger King, Coffee Primo, Eat In, KFC. Children's play area. Campervan access.

M25 Junction 24

Trent Park *EN4 0PS*

Getting there

From Junction 24 take the A111 Cockfosters and continue past West Lodge Hotel. After the tourist sign for Trent Country Park 300 yards look for the entrance on the left, just after a bend through an imposing, but unmarked, gateway.

Return to M25 Junction 24

Turn right from the park entrance to the A111 and return to the M25 as signed.

Walk

This is an orderly and well tended country park, with hard surface paths creating accessibility routes and clean all-weather walking. The London Loop walk starts by the car park and the route is shown on an informative notice board. There is plenty of space to go off-path and enjoy the shade of the ancient spreading trees in this generously sized estate.

Facilities

Free parking 0830 to dusk. WC+disabled, visitor centre, café with outdoor seating, picnic tables, water garden and children's activities. Free dog poo bags from visitor centre. Campervan access.

Getting there

From Junction 28 take the A1023 Brentwood. Turn left almost immediately, signed South Weald. In the village of South Weald bear left, Weald Road, and the entrance to the car park is signed to the right.

Return to M25 Junction 28

Turn left out of the car park onto Weald Road. Bear right in South Weald. At the A1023 turn right. The M25 intersection is directly ahead.

Walk

With nearly 500 acres of parkland, including lakes and avenues of mature trees, Weald Park is an attractive place to ramble.
There are no formal walking trails, just a huge amount of green space. Wildlife flourishes in these undisturbed surroundings, and deer can often be spotted at dusk.

Facilities

P&D car park £2.00. Tax exempt vehicles free. 0800-1700. WC+disabled, refreshments, visitor centre, animal centre, Information board. All Terrain Tramper Scooter hire from visitor centre. Campervan access.

Thorndon Country Park *CM13 3RZ*

Getting there

From Junction 29 take the A127 Basildon, Southend. Turn left for the A128, Brentwood. Pass through Herongate and Ingrave, and turn left at the tourist signpost to Thorndon Country Park North, The Avenue.

Return to M25 Junction 29

Return to the A128, turning right from The Avenue. At the roundabout, take the A127 Romford to rejoin the M25 at the next roundabout.

Walk

There are two signed routes.

The Wildside Walk (yellow signs) is a 5 mile route around the park. To reach the start point, follow the bridleway from the car park and turn left at the lake. At the Wildside Walk marker bear left to follow the signs. On the return leg, remember to turn left on the Bridleway to get back to the car park.

A shorter option is to take the bridleway from the car park, through the Octagon Plantation and then turn right on the public footpath (red markers). Carry on to the boundary of the wood, and then turn left. Pass through woodland, continuing straight at the crossroads of paths, to the Old Park. Then turn left onto a path shared with the Wildside Walk until returning to the Bridleway. Pass the lake to the left on the return to the car park.

Facilities

P&D car park £2.00. WC+disabled, visitor centre, picnic tables, refreshments, shop, map and information board. Campervan access.

RM15 4XJ Belhus Woods Country Park

Getting there
From Junction 31, and at the roundabout, take the Aveley exit, Ship Lane. In Aveley turn left at a mini-roundabout (High Street). At the next mini-roundabout turn right, Mill Road.
At a roundabout take exit 2, Upminster. After a mile turn right into Belhus Woods Country Park.

Return to M25 Junction 31
Turn left from the car park and take exit 2 at the roundabout to return to Aveley. Turn left at the first mini-roundabout to High Street, and right at the next mini-roundabout onto Ship Lane.
Continue to Junction 31. Follow signs to the M25 Gatwick (southbound) or Dartford Crossing A282 (northbound).

Walk
Three walk routes are signposted around the park. The Blue route is 2km, the Brown route 2.5km and the Red route 3km. All routes start through the gates near the visitor centre.
An information board gives a huge amount of detail about each track, including the steepness or otherwise. The Blue route is flat, with a wide accessible track.
Formerly a country estate, the woodland is restful and tranquil.

Facilities
P&D car park £2.00, tax exempt vehicles free, open 0800-dusk. WC, visitor centre, light refreshments. Campervan access.

M27

From New Forest to Portsmouth

Junction

Half Moon Common

Getting there

From Junction 2 take the A36 Salisbury. At the next roundabout take the A36 Salisbury. There are services on this roundabout. Enter Wellow. Turn left, signed Bramshaw, Black Hill Road. Cross a cattle grid and the car park is on the left.

Return to M27 Junction 2

Turn right out of the car park. At the T-junction turn right, Southampton A36. At the roundabout take exit 3, signed Southampton, M27 to rejoin the motorway.

Walk

Walk onto the Common from the car park onto a wide swathe of grass between the trees and bracken. There are no marked paths, and no navigational difficulties in heading away from the road into the lush woodland. As a general indication, bear rightwards rather than leftwards to stay clear of the nearby golf and cricket areas.
There's scope here for a long walk if time and weather permit.

Facilities

Free parking. Campervan access.
Services on the A36 roundabout, with WC, café, petrol.

M27 Junction 5

Itchen Valley Country Park *SO30 3HQ*

Getting there

From Junction 5 take the A335, Southampton. Turn left at the traffic lights. At a roundabout take exit 2, Mansbridge Road. At the next roundabout take exit 1, Allington Lane. Continue to Itchen Valley Country Park on the left.

Return to M27 Junction 5

Turn right out of the park. At the mini-roundabout, go straight on. At the next roundabout, take exit 3, A27 Eastleigh. Enter Southampton and at the next roundabout take exit 2, Eastleigh. Turn right at the traffic lights, signed London A335 and return to the M27.

Walk

There are five marked trails in the park to satisfy the needs of walkers, all starting from the visitor centre.

The 30 minute Paw Trail is designed for dogs. It's a leafy, well-maintained path that includes a large open area for ball games.

The Forest Trail is an easy access path. Other trails of varying lengths meander through the 400 acres of parkland.

Facilities

P&D car park 0830 to dusk. WC+disabled, café, visitor centre, children's play area, electric scooter hire from visitor centre, dog poo bags (10p) from visitor centre. Campervan access.

SO31 1BH Manor Farm Country Park

Getting there

From Junction 8 follow signs to Manor Farm Country Park. Take the second right turn, Rylands Lane, to enter the park.

Return to M27 Junction 8

Leave the grounds of the park and turn left, signed M27, and return to the motorway.

Walk

With four car parks and many walk routes Manor Farm is worth several visits.

From the farm and visitor centre car park, walk to a footpath sign by the entrance. Two paths start from this point. One is the Barnsfield path which leads to refreshments and a river. The other path, marked with a red arrow, is a rural route running between fields, and it's up to you to decide how far you want to go and then turn round.

Dog walkers not visiting the farm are encouraged to use one of the earlier car parks.

Facilities

Parking charge on entry £1.50 weekdays, £2.00 weekends and Bank Holidays. Working farm admission separate. WC+disabled, café, visitor centre, picnic area, working farm museum, children's activities, dog water. Accessible trails. Maps available from entry point and visitor centre. Campervan access.

M27 Junction 9

Botley Wood *PO15 7LJ*

Getting there

From Junction 9 follow signs to Whiteley, Outlet shopping. At a roundabout take exit 2, signed Outlet Shopping, Whiteley Way. Enter the Shopping Village and park near the entrance.

Return to M27 Junction 9

Leave the shopping village and take exit 2 at the roundabout, signed M27 and rejoin the motorway at the next roundabout.

Walk

Leave the shopping village and cross to the other side of the roundabout to a blue pedestrian sign. Turn right on a tarmac path across a small bridge. Then turn left onto a gravel track.

At a waymark post, covered in yellow arrows and mostly hidden behind a hawthorn bush, turn right. Follow this wide track to enter Whiteley Pastures. Once here, it is as if the outlet village never existed.

This woodland is home to Hampshire's largest nightingale population, so keep your ears open for their distinctive song. Follow the track for half your walk time, and then return the same way.

Facilities

Free parking. Shopping facilities, including picnic supplies and ATMs. Guide Dogs only in the shopping areas. Pet dogs are welcome on the terrace of Frankie and Bennies close to the entrance. Campervan access.

M40

From London to Birmingham, via Oxford

Junction

Burnham Beeches

Getting there

From Junction 2 take the A355 Slough. Enter Farnham Common and take the 3rd right turn after an infant school, Beeches Road. Go straight at a crossroads to enter Burnham Beeches car park.

Return to M40 Junction 2

Return to the A355 and then turn left to rejoin to the motorway.

Walk

Burnham Beeches gives West Londoners a recreation space in 540 acres of ancient woodland.

One short walk route is to go straight through the trees from the car park as far as the Withy Spring following a clear path to cross the stream. At an intersection of paths turn right. Cross Sir Henry Peter's Drive and continue in the same direction to cross 'The Heath'. This path leads down to the Upper Pond. Bear right on one of the many paths to return to the car park.

The wheelchair accessible path starts at the information point, where full details are available.

Facilities

Free parking. WC+disabled. Refreshments, and ice cream van in summer. Information centre with maps and walk routes. Free poo bags at car park. Dog Code in force to protect trees and soil. Campervan access.

Spade Oak Nature Reserve

Getting there

From Junction 4 take the A404 Marlow. Bear left, A4155, signed Marlow, Bourne End and continue to Little Marlow. Enter Bourne End and turn right, Coldmoorholme Lane, to reach The Spade Oak car park.

Return to M40 Junction 4

Turn right from the car park. At the T-junction, turn left. Take exit 1 at the mini-roundabout. Continue to a roundabout and take exit 3, A4010 Aylesbury to return to the M40.

Walk

This is a 45 minute circular walk without stiles.

From the car park turn right and then left at a public footpath sign. Follow the footpath arrow to the right before a metal kissing gate. Walk parallel to the lane for a short distance.

Cross a wooden footbridge and turn left at the next footpath sign. Walk through one field with the hedge on the left and into the next field. Follow the path into woodland on the left. Cross a metal footbridge and take the yellow permissive path to the left. At the lake turn left.

Shortly after a picnic table and lifebuoy follow a yellow marker over a footbridge to the left. Cross a field, and go through the kissing gate to return to The Spade Oak.

Facilities

At the Spade Oak (01628 520090), food served 1200-2200. A sophisticated traditional village pub with gastro menu. Well-behaved dogs on leads are welcome in the garden seating area. Dog water provided.

Cowleaze Woods

Getting there
From Junction 5 take the A40 Stokenchurch. Immediately turn left, signed A40 Lewknor, Oxford. Turn left, signed Christmas Common, Chiltern Sculpture Trail. Turn left into the Cowleaze Woods Forestry Commission car park.

Return to M40 Junction 5
Turn right from the car park. At the junction turn right, A40 and continue to return to the M40.

Walk
Walk away from the road on one of the many paths to a broad swathe of grass, which seems to be the playground of choice for many local dogs.

Within the wood there are many paths to choose from to enjoy a very satisfying 30-40 minute ramble. In Spring Cowleaze Woods is awash with bluebells.

Facilities
Free parking, 6ft 6 height restriction.

At The Leathern Bottle (01844 351482; OX49 5TW) in nearby Lewknor. Food served Mon-Fri 1200-1400, 1900-2130; Saturday 1800-2200, Sunday 1900-2130. Reservations recommended at weekends. Children's play area, beer garden. Dogs are welcome in the pub, dog water provided.

OX49 5NF **Cuxham**

Getting there

From Junction 6 take the B4009 signed Watlington. Pass through Shipburn and enter Watlington. At a T-junction turn right, B480 Cuxham. At a roundabout take exit 2, unsigned. Enter Cuxham, and park at The Half Moon on the right. The car park is gated.

Return to M40 Junction 6

Turn left from the car park and enter Watlington. Take exit 2 at the roundabout. At a give-way sign turn left, signed High Wycombe. Turn left, B4009 signed Chinnor and M40 to rejoin the motorway.

Walk

Turn right out of the car park and turn left at a green footpath sign to Manor Farm. Continue on this farm track as it leads up the hill, getting steeper and steeper as you go.
This is a one track walk, so continue with the hedge on the right and fields on either side for half your walk time, and then return the same way.

Facilities

At The Half Moon (01491 614151), a 17th century traditional thatched inn. Well-behaved dogs are welcome inside and in the garden. Disabled access buzzer. Campervan access.

M40 Junction 7

Northbound only

Great Haseley *OX44 7JQ*

Getting there

From Junction 7 take the A329 Wallingford. Turn left, signed Great Haseley. In Great Haseley turn right, signed Great Milton, Rectory Road. Park at The Plough Inn on the left.

Return to M40 Northbound

Turn right from car park and left at the T-junction signed Thame. At the next T-junction turn right, unsigned. Turn left, signed Birmingham M40, Oxford A40. At a roundabout take exit 2 and continue to rejoin the M40.

Walk

Turn left out of the car park and walk to a green footpath sign by Horseclose Cottages. Follow this arrow, cross an access road and continue into a field onto a well trodden path. Continue through a gate and across a road towards a church. Walk through the churchyard and turn left, at an arrow.

At a recreation ground carry straight on and continue into the next field for an entirely rural romp in the Chilterns. Continue to follow the arrows and turn round to retrace the route.

Great Haseley has featured more than once in the Midsomer Murders TV series.

Facilities

At The Plough (01844 279283). Food served 1200-1400; 1900-2130. Dogs are welcome in the bar. Campervan access.

Oxford motorway services are on the return route.

OX25 3QH **Weston on the Green**

Getting there
From Junction 9 take the A34 Oxford. Turn left, signed Middleton Stoney B430. Drive over the dual carriageway, and at a mini-roundabout turn left, signed motorway. Park at The Chequers Country Inn on the right.

Return to M40 Junction 9
Turn right out of the car park, and turn left onto the dual carriageway, signed A34, M40 to return to the motorway.

Walk
Climb a stile to the rear of the bar entrance to enter a field. Walk with the car park fence on the left, and when this runs out turn right. Continue to a gate with a yellow way-marker and through a copse in a half left direction to a kissing gate and walk half left across a field to a metal gate in the far corner. Cross a wooden footbridge and then follow the arrow half-right into a field. Aim for the wooden gate ahead, where a further arrow points into woodland to the left. Turn round at a wooden footbridge for a 30 minute walk.

Facilities
At The Chequers (01869 351743). All day menu 1200-2130. Well-behaved dogs on leads are welcome in the bar and garden. Dog water is provided. Campervan access.

M40 Junction 10

Cherwell Valley Services *OX27 7RD*

Getting there

Leave the M40 at Junction 10 and follow the signs to park at Cherwell Valley Services.

Return to M40 Junction 10

Leave the services area and follow signs to rejoin the M40.

Walk

Follow the path between the Travelodge and the services over a wooden bridge. Turn right onto the short grass, with a field on the left and a stream on the right. At the end of the field return to the stream on an overgrown path.

Walk with the stream on the right to a T-junction of paths. Turn left and continue over a footbridge and through the trees with woodland to the left and a hedge on the right into a field. Bear left at the fencing and through a gateway. At this point the stream should be on the right. Continue as far as a dog poo bin and turn right to return to the car park.

In wet weather wellies are essential for this walk.

Facilities

Moto motorway service facilities, Costa, M&S, Upper Crust, Burger King, Thorntons. Children's play area. Showers. ATM. Travelodge motel. Campervan access.

Getting there

From Junction 11 take the A422 Brackley. At a roundabout take exit 3, A422 Buckingham, Milton Keynes. Turn left, signed Middleton Cheney. Park at The New Inn on the left.

Return to M40 Junction 11

Return to the A422 and turn right, signed Banbury. Continue on the A422 to return to the M40.

Walk

Turn right from the car park to a footpath sign to Thenford and walk down a paved driveway. Climb a stile at the footpath sign on the left and walk forward with Middleton Farm on the right. Cross the next stile and head towards the trees.

Climb another stile and follow the arrow slightly to the right across two fields. Go through a gate and stile to follow the arrow pointing to the right. Turn left at the corner of the field turn, and through a metal gate. Turn left and immediately left again through a gate into a copse with a pool. Turn round here for a 35 minute walk.

Facilities

At The New Inn (01295 712029). Meals and snacks served 1200-1430. Look out for experts playing Aunt Sally, a traditional pub game in the Banbury area. Well-behaved dogs are welcome in the bar. Campervan access.

Hatton Locks CV35 7JL

Getting there
From Junction 15 take the A46 Coventry. Turn left, Solihull A4177 and continue to Hatton. Turn left on a hill, signed Hatton Locks and car park.

Return to M40 Junction 15
From the car park turn right. At the roundabout take exit 2, A4177 Warwick. At the next roundabout, take exit 3 A46, signed M40, Birmingham and rejoin the M40 at the Longbridge roundabout.

Walk
Cross the canal bridge and turn right onto the Grand Union canal for a glorious walk along the towpath and the chance to watch narrowboats climbing the 21 closely placed locks of the 'Stairway to Heaven', or Hatton Flight.
Pass the café and shop on the left and walk past two winding holes as far as Bridge No.55, which is a good turning point for a 30 minute walk.

Facilities
P&D car park £1.00 open 0730 to dusk. WC, café with outdoor seating, shop. Campervan access.
At The Waterman (01926 492427). All day menu. Dogs welcome in the large garden.

B95 5GD

Henley in Arden

Getting there

Exit at Junction 16 and turn right. Continue to Henley in Arden, A3400. At the end of the town turn left, Warwick Road, and turn left after a petrol station, Prince Harry Drive, to a car park.

Return to M40 Junction 15 Southbound

Turn left at the end of Prince Harry Drive, Warwick Road. Continue through Claverdon village, and turn right where signed to the M40 at the Longbridge roundabout.

Walk

Pass a children's play area and cross a metal footbridge. Turn left towards a church, and then right through a kissing gate. Walk uphill and bear left to walk parallel to the churchyard, through a copse of trees and downhill to join a path at the bottom of the slope. Turn right and circle round the foot of The Mount, a motte and bailey site, for a 30 minute walk.

Facilities

There are many 16th century hostelries and cafes on Henley High Street, many with outdoor seating in summer. Also a Somerfield supermarket and several delis for picnic fare.

The Blue Bell (01564 793049; B95 5QP) gastro-pub serves meals and bar snacks 1130-1430, 1800-2230. Dogs welcome in the bar and at outside tables.

The Crabmill, Preston Bagot (01926 843342; B95 5EE) Lunch and bar meals from 1200. Dogs welcome in the bar and garden.

M42

Birmingham semi-orbital

Junction

B45 8ER **The Lickey Hills**

Getting there

From Junction 1 take the B4096 Rednal and Lickey, exit 4. Continue for just over a mile, pass a Texaco garage, and turn right at the Lickey Hills sign, Warren Lane.

Return to M5 Junction 4

From Warren Lane turn left on the B4096. Drive back to the M42 roundabout and take the 4th exit Birmingham A46, M5. Continue on the A46 to join the M5 at Junction 4.

Walk

There are three trails at the Lickey Hills. The Squirrel Trail is the shortest at just under a mile, the Bluebell Trail is 1.5 miles, and the Woodpecker Trail an enthusiastic 7 miles. All the trails are clearly marked and very easy to follow.

The Lickeys were JRR Tolkien's inspiration for Middle Earth in The Hobbit and The Lord of the Rings. He is said to have known every inch of the landscape, and every detail of the trees and plants here.

Facilities

Free car park, closes at dusk. WC, visitor centre, shop, café with outdoor seating, large children's play area and child-friendly displays about the park. Campervan access.

Earlswood Lakes *B94 5SL*

Getting there

From Junction 4 take the A3400, Henley in Arden. Turn right at a roundabout, signed Illshaw Heath, Kineton Lane. At a T-junction turn right, signed Earlswood, Cut-Throat Lane. Turn right, signed Earlswood. At a crossroads, turn left and immediately right to park at The Reservoir Hotel.

Return to M42 Junction 4

Turn left from the car park, and immediately right. Bear left, Cut Throat Lane. Take the third left turn, and continue ahead onto Kineton Lane. At the roundabout, take exit 1 A3400, Solihull and return to the M42.

Walk

This walk takes you around the perimeter of the 'Windmill Pool' and is flat, easy walking.
Leave the car park and turn left, Valley Road. Turn left at a wooden kissing gate. Follow the path around the lake and turn round after 15-20 minutes for a 30 to 40 minute walk.

Facilities

At The Reservoir (01564 702220). Food served from 1200. Budget menu with a focus on families. Children's play area, and Wacky Warehouse (entry charge). Dogs allowed at one tiny patio table overlooking the car park. Campervan access.

B76 0DY Kingsbury Water Park

Getting there

From Junction 9 take the A4097, signed Kingsbury Water Park.

At the roundabout, take exit 1 (Coton Road). Continue ahead, and the entrance to Kingsbury Water Park is signed on the right.

Return to M42 Junction 9

Turn left out of the car park and at the roundabout take exit 3. Continue ahead to return to the motorway.

Walk

This park is a planning miracle, created out of spent gravel pits. There are fifteen lakes in 620 acres of leisure space, and many of the paths are surfaced so it's fine all weather and accessible walking.

Maps and info are available from the visitor centre, but essentially this is a space where it is very comfortable to amble around the lakes and woodland without a fixed plan. Dog swimming is popular from the little lakeside beaches, away from the watersports lakes.

Facilities

Car park (£3.00). Open 0830 to dusk. WC+disabled. Visitor centre, cafe, shop, adventure playground, picnic site, miniature railway. Access paths, mobility scooter hire (01827 872660). Campervan access.

Appleby Magna DE12 7AH

Getting there

From Junction 11 take the Measham exit. Turn right, signed Appleby Magna, Rectory Lane. At a T-junction with Measham Road, turn right into Church Street. Pass a church, and park at The Black Horse on the right.

Return to M42 Junction 11

Pass the church and turn left into Rectory Lane. At the T-junction turn left, and rejoin the motorway at the following roundabout.

Walk

Turn onto Black Horse Hill and turn right at a footpath sign to the left of 'Apple Tree House'. Keep a hedge on the right and continue to the corner of the field, passing a couple of yellow footpath arrows.

Follow a blue arrow to the left, through a gate, and then half left through the centre of the crops in the field ahead. Follow a yellow arrow through a gap in the hedgerow, and then turn left into the next field towards a yellow marker ahead. Cross a small footbridge to enter the next field, and follow the path through the crop.

At the end of the field aim for a yellow-topped post, and turn left on Black Horse Hill to return to the pub.

Facilities

At the 16th century Black Horse (01530 270588). Lunch served 1230-1430; 1830-2130 Tues-Sun. Dogs welcome in the bar, and at the outdoor tables. Campervan access.

M48 and M50

Welsh Borders and The Severn Estuary

M48

Junction

M50

M48 Junction 1

Severn View Services *BS35 4BH*

Getting there
Access Severn View Services as signed from the motorway.

Return to M48 Junction 1
Return to the motorway as signed.

Walk
Severn View services sit right on the long distance Severn Way path, so this walk couldn't be easier to fit into your journey.

Walk past the Travelodge to skirt the base of a grassy knoll towards an office building and a waymark post. Turn right into woodland. Follow the path downwards, and round to the right.

At a wooden kissing gate go straight, into a field, walking with the River Severn on the left to the next kissing gate. There's a good view of the estuary and Severn Bridge from here.

Walk through the next field, with a small tower to the right. From here the line of the path is clear to see as it drops down a small but steep hill to the next gate. Continue on this path, always with the river to the left, until your halfway point and then turn round to return.

Facilities
Moto motorway services, Burger King, Costa. Dogs allowed at outside tables. Free parking for 2 hours. Campervan access.

Getting there

From Junction 2 take the A466 Chepstow. Continue on the A466 to reach Tintern Abbey and car park.

Return to M48 Junction 2

Turn left from the car park and continue on the A466 to return to the motorway.

Walk

Walk towards the river and turn left, with the river to the right. Follow the signed Tintern Trail footpath to cross a footbridge over the river and turn right. The path now is a broad swathe of green meadow land. Reverse the route to return to Tintern Abbey.

Facilities

At Tintern Abbey. Free car park for pub and tea room customers. Public WC+disabled.

At The Anchor (01291 689207) all day food and snacks are available. Small general stores in tea rooms. Well-behaved dogs on leads welcome in the large garden areas.

Abbey open 0930-1730 (1800 in summer). Entry £3.60. Only assistance dogs are permitted inside the ruins. Campervan access.

M50 Junction 1

Twyning *GL20 6FL*

Getting there
From Junction 1 follow signs to Twyning. Enter Twyning and park in The Fleet Inn car park.

Return to M50 Junction 1
Turn right from the car park and rejoin the M50 as signed.

Walk
Turn left from the car park and walk down to the River Avon. Turn right at the river onto the waymarked river path, climbing over one stile at the start.
Walk along the wide grassy track with the river to the left to your halfway point, and then turn round to return to the car park.
This is a perfect hot weather walk over cooling grass. Pleasure boats pass by from time to time, and the atmosphere is very relaxing.

Facilities
At the 15th century Fleet Inn (01684 274310). Food served 1200-1430; 1800-2200. Outside seating area overlooking the river. Children's playground. Well behaved dogs on leads are welcome in the bar area. Dog water provided. Campervan access.

Getting there

From Junction 2 take the A417, Ledbury. Turn left, signed Bromsberrow Heath, Beach Lane. Continue straight until a crossroads at Greenway, and turn left, B4216. Enter Dymock and park near The Beaumont Arms.

Return to M50 Junction 2

Turn left by the pub, signed Ledbury B4216. Turn right, signed Broome Green, Bromsberrow and continue through these villages. At a T-junction turn right, signed M50, Gloucester A417 to return to the M50.

Walk

Join the waymarked Daffodil Way opposite the Beauchamp Arms. Walk through two meadows full of wild flowers and over a small brook. Follow the path through a metal gate into a large farmed field and turn left to walk around the field with the hedgerow to the left.

Continue on the broad track as far as the telephone wires and a clump of trees and for a 30-40 minute walk turn around here.

If time permits, there is an interesting display about the Dymock poets inside the church.

Facilities

At The Beauchamp Arms (01531 890266), community owned pub with bar food available 1200-1400. Dogs welcome at the outside tables.

Dymock Forest

Getting there

From Junction 3 take the B4221 signed Newent, Gorsley. Turn left just after the Roadmaker Inn into Ivy House Lane. Take the second left turn, passing the 'The Larches'. At a T-junction turn left. The unsigned entrance to the Forestry Commission car park is on the right.

Return to M50 Junction 3

Turn left from the car park, and then turn right, Swagwater Lane. Turn right at a T-junction, and then turn right at the next T-junction by the Roadmaker Inn and return to the M50.

Walk

This is walking country at its best, through woodland maintained by the Forestry Commission. There are no signed trails, but the paths are clear and easy to follow.
The path from the right side of the car park gives a fine view over the valley and the wooded hills beyond. It's easy to lose all sense of time here, so if you have a schedule to keep set an alarm!

Facilities

Free car park in Dymock Forest. Campervan access.
At the Roadmaker Inn (01989 720352; HR9 7SW) in Gorsley, run by a team of Gurkhas, with Gurkha food a speciality. Open from 1130. Dogs permitted at tables on the small outdoor patio.

Getting there

Continue from the M50 on the A40 Monmouth to the Wilton roundabout. Turn left, signed B4260 Wilton. Take the first right, Wilton Lane, before the bridge and park at The White Lion.

Return to M50 Junction 4

To return to the M50, take exit 4, A40, from the Wilton roundabout to join the motorway.

Walk

Walk along the lane for a short distance, passing the Wilton Court Hotel on the right, to a stile and footpath sign on the left. Go over the stile (with dog hole) and follow the clear path along the river bank over three fields. Then return the same way.

Dog swimming is possible from the rear garden of the White Lion where there is some protection from the strong current of the River Wye.

Facilities

The White Lion (01989 562785) is a popular 17th century inn with a good Bistro style menu. Well-behaved dogs are welcome in the bar and rear gardens. Campervan access.

The Northwest Motorways

M56

From Manchester to Chester

Junction

M57

From the M62 to Liverpool North

M60

Manchester Orbital

M23 0BA Wythenshawe Park

Getting there
From Junction 2 take exit 2, M6 Birmingham. At the next roundabout take exit 2, M6 Birmingham. At the next roundabout take exit 3, Wythenshawe Park and A5103. Merge and stay in the left hand lane. At the traffic lights turn left, and turn left at the sign for Wythenshawe Park. Drive through the grounds to reach the car park on the right.

Return to M56 Southbound
Exit the park and turn right. Continue straight at the first and second traffic lights, signed M56 Chester, Warrington. Turn right onto the A5103, signed M56, Chester and follow the signs to return to the M56.

Walk
There are 250 acres of parkland here, so plenty of space for exercise in this island of calm amidst the transport network. Cromwell's troops occupied this estate in the early 1600s and there's now a Cromwell statue near the hall. This marks the area where local dog owners seem to exercise their hounds.
Trails are not signed in the park, but helpful maps are available at the visitor centre.

Facilities
Free parking, WC+disabled, café, visitor centre, wardens on duty. Campervan access.

Styal Country Park *SK9 4LA*

Getting there
Leave the M56 at Junction 5 following the motorway 'leg' and take exit 2 at the roundabout. At the next roundabout take exit 2, B5166 Cheadle, Styal Country Park. Enter Wythenshawe. At a T-junction turn right, signed Styal Country Park, B5166, Styal Road. Turn right at a tourist sign to enter Styal Country Park.

Return to M56 Junction 5
Exit the car park and turn right. Enter Wythenshawe, and turn left at the traffic lights, signed M56. At the roundabout take exit 1, signed M56/Airport. At the next roundabout take exit 2 to return to the motorway.

Walk
A nineteenth century cotton mill is not the obvious place for a walk, but amongst the traces of industrial Manchester there's 380 acres of country park too.
Leave the car park and go through a wooden kissing gate on the left. This is a waymarked footpath to Wilmslow. Follow the yellow arrows to cross the fields on a well-trodden path. Then reverse the route to return to the car park.
The National Trust exhibitions are worth a visit, but no dogs are permitted and there's restricted access for pushchairs.

Facilities
Car Park £4.00, NT members free. WC, restaurant, NT shop. Separate charges to visit the mill and exhibitions. Campervan access.

Lindow Common

Getting there

From Junction 6 take the A538 Wilmslow. At the roundabout continue, A538 Wilmslow. Pass The Boddington and Dragon on the right and immediately turn right, and then quickly left into the unsigned car park for Lindow Common.

Return to M56 Junction 6

Turn right from the car park and left at the T-junction, A538. At the roundabout take exit 1, M56 to return to the motorway.

Walk

There are well maintained paths leading into the heathland, and the most obvious path from the car park leads deliciously deeper into the heather.

This is an area to wander around at will, enjoying the feel of this timeless common land.

Lindow Moss, next to the Common, is famous for the Iron Age body preserved in its peat, but the marsh is not safe for walkers.

Facilities

Free parking.

At the Boddington & Dragon Arms (01625 525849; SK9 5LR). Traditional food served 1130-2130, Thai menu evenings. Children welcome until 2000. Dogs outside only. Wi-Fi access.

Dunham Massey Hall *WA14 4SJ*

Getting there

From Junction 7 take the A56 Altrincham and Dunham Massey. At a roundabout take exit 3, Dunham Massey. At the traffic lights turn left, B5160, Charcoal Road. Turn left as signed for Dunham Massey Hall.

Return to M56

Exit Dunham Massey and turn right. At the traffic lights turn right, signed M56.

Walk

A National Trust property, Dunham Massey Hall dominates its 250 acre park. Guided tours available, exhibitions and Winter Garden. Entry charges apply. Assistance dogs are welcome in all parts of the house and grounds. A free walks leaflet is provided, detailing the many trails throughout the park grounds.

For dog walkers, the woods surrounding the picnic area and have been designated off-lead dog walking space. Dogs must be on lead elsewhere as deer roam throughout the park.

Facilities

Parking charge £4.00, NT free, open 0900 to dusk. WC+disabled, restaurant, kiosk, picnic tables, NT shop. Mobility scooter hire (0161 941 1025). Campervan access.

Walton Hall

Getting there

From Junction 11 take the A56 Warrington. Enter Walton. At the traffic lights turn right, signed Walton Hall and gardens. Turn right at the Walton Arms and continue to the car park.

Return to M56 Junction 11

Turn left at the Walton Arms. At the traffic lights, turn left, signed M56, Runcorn. At the roundabout take exit 1, N. Wales M56 and return to the motorway.

Walk

Walton Hall and gardens are the main attraction for visitors and fully accessible paths and facilities are found here. The gardens are reached from the left hand side of the car park entrance. Families flock here in the school holidays to enjoy the outdoor games, zoo and play areas, or to ramble through the extensive parkland.

The dog walk route lies outside the park, on the Bridgewater Canal tow path adjoining the car park. Turn left to walk along the cool and leafy path. This is considerably quieter than the hall and an ideal walk for those seeking some peace and quiet.

Facilities

P&D gated car park open 0800 to dusk. Visitor centre, WC+disabled, café, gift shop, children's activities. Campervan access.

M57 Junction 1

Stadt Moers Country Park

Getting there

From Junction 1 turn to Whiston, eastbound exit 3, westbound exit 6. At the traffic lights turn left, Huyton, and the unsigned entrance to Stadt Moers Park is on the left before a bridge.

Return to M57 Junction 1

Turn right from the car park and turn right at the traffic lights, signed Whiston Station. Continue to return to the motorway.

Walk

Stadt Moers Park has been regenerated from waste land and is now a thriving natural environment with meadows, woodland and ponds all criss-crossed by footpaths and spread over 220 acres. The paths are clearly colour coded, and include circular routes suitable for wheelchairs.

To reach the main part of the park, go past the Environment Centre and through a tunnel under the motorway to the starting point for all the trails.

Facilities

Free parking, visitor centre, WC+disabled (when visitor centre is open), and possibly the largest dog poo bin in the UK in the car park. Campervan access.

L12 0HB Croxteth Hall and Country Park

Getting there

From Junction 4 take the A5207, St Helens. At traffic lights, turn left A580, Liverpool. At the next traffic lights turn left, West Derby, Stonebridge Lane. Continue through a housing development and turn right at the traffic lights. Turn left at a roundabout, and the gates to Croxteth Park are on the left.

Return to M57 Junction 4

Turn right from the park and then take exit 3 at the roundabout, Croxteth. At the traffic lights turn right A580, signed St Helens. Continue and follow M57 signs to return to the motorway.

Walk

Croxteth Hall sits in over 500 acres of parkland with miles of trails marked throughout the park.
The River Trail is a hard surfaced wheelchair and buggy friendly path that starts at the main Hall.

Facilities

Free parking, WC+disabled, café, children's play areas, Jungle Parc, adventure playground, walled garden, gift shop. Park opens 0700-2000 summer, 0700-1800 winter. Campervan access.

M60 Junction 6

Trafford Water Park

Getting there

From Junction 6 follow signs to Trafford Watersports. At a roundabout take exit 2, Trafford Water Park and continue to the car park.

Return to M60 Junction 6

Leave the car park and return to the M60 as signed at the roundabouts.

Walk

There are three trails in Trafford Water Park, all well signed from the visitor centre. The first trail, Chorlton Water Park Trail can be joined by walking down to the River Mersey and then turning right to follow the marked path (2 miles approx). The Sale Water Park route (3 miles) starts at the car park, and leads around the perimeter of the lake to the River Mersey. This path comes closest to the visitor centre and facilities.

Another possibility is simply to walk down to the river, and follow the riverbank path for as long as you want. Dogs are discouraged from the Priory Gardens Trail to protect nesting birds.

Facilities

Free car park (gated), WC, café, picnic area. Campervan access.

M27 6NG **Clifton Country Park**

Getting there
From Junction 16 turn right, A666 Kearsley. Continue to a brown sign for Clifton Country Park and turn right, Clifton House Road. Turn right at the next sign to the car park.

Return to M60 Southbound
Leave the car park and turn left at the crossroads. At the T-junction turn right, A666. Enter Kearsley and continue on the A666 Bolton. At a roundabout, take exit 1 to join the M61 (Salford, Manchester, M60). Towards Junction 1 move into the right hand lane. Follow signs to Liverpool, Birmingham to merge onto the M60 southbound.

Walk
Clifton Country Park, set in the Irwell Valley, is a haven of calm with air pungent with the scent of wild flowers in summer.
There are several trails: The Perimeter Trail (easy) is 2.5km, the Wet Earth Trail 3.5km and the Lake Trail 4.5km.
The path circling the lake is hard surfaced and accessible to wheelchair users.

Facilities
Free gated car park 0930 to dusk. Visitor centre open 1300 to 1700 weekdays, 0930-1700 weekends. WC (visitor centre hours). Children's play area. Free dog poo bags from visitor centre. Campervan access.

Heaton Park

Getting there

From Junction 19 take the A576 Manchester City Centre and Heaton Hall and Park, eastbound exit 3, westbound exit 1. Turn right at the traffic lights, A6044. Enter Prestwich and turn right, signed Lakes car park.

Return to M60 Junction 19

Exit the park grounds and turn left. At the traffic lights turn left A576, Rochdale. Continue to return to the M60.

Walk

With 600 acres of parkland, Heaton Park is a massively popular open space for Mancunians as the huge car park suggests. As this is also a venue for large scale open-air concerts and events, the road-weary hound may despair of a tree and piece of ground to call his own amongst all the municipal merry making during the school holidays.

For a quiet stroll, walk around the edge of the lake to reach the Hall and facilities. Continue to walk to the front of the Hall to find an open area where the doggie people are. There is plenty of space here to relax and take in the view of Manchester and the Pennines beyond.

Facilities

Free car park, closes at dusk. WC+disabled, cafes, visitor centre, children's play areas, pets corner and show farm, rowing boat hire, tram museum, garden centre. Campervan access.

Alkrington Woods

Getting there

From Junction 20 turn left, A644 Middleton. Enter Middleton.
At the next two roundabouts take exit 1, A576 Bury. Alkrington Woods car park is signed to the left. Alternative parking in a lay-by further on the left, with direct access to the woods.

Return to M60 Eastbound

Turn right from the car park, A576. At the roundabout continue A576 Oldham. At the next roundabout take exit 3, A664 Manchester. At the traffic lights turn left, M60 Oldham. At the next roundabout take exit 3, M60. Enter Chadderton. Turn left at the traffic lights, M60. Continue in the right hand lane to turn right onto the M60 where signed.

Walk

Alkrington Woods is a local nature reserve occupying the grounds of the former Alkrington Hall Estate. Several marked and graded trails encourage walkers to meander through the woodland.
There are two easy all-access 1.5 mile routes with white or blue posts, a medium 1.5 mile route with yellow posts, and a 3.5 mile route marked in red.

Facilities

Free car parking. Information board with trail routes. Picnic tables. Campervan access.

Daisy Nook Country Park *OL7 9JY*

Getting there

From Junction 23 follow signs for the A635, Ashton-under-Lyne. Enter Ashton-under-Lyne. At a roundabout take exit 1 Oldham. At the traffic lights, turn left A627, Oldham Road. At the next traffic lights turn left, Newmarket Road. Turn right, signed Daisy Nook Garden Centre, and the entrance to the park is on the right.

Return to M60 Junction 23

Leave the car park and turn left. At the T-junction turn left, A627 Ashton-under-Lyne. At the traffic lights turn right, signed M60, to follow signs back to the motorway.

Walk

This is a gem of a walk. There are so many paths that it must be possible to visit Daisy Nook a hundred times and never repeat a route.

One of the main features is the Hollinwood Branch providing flat, level walking over a disused canal.

The Oldham Way and the Tameside Trail routes also go through the park.

Facilities

Free parking, visitor centre, WC+disabled (visitor centre hours), café, shop, children's play area, picnic areas. Campervan access.

SK5 7HE Reddish Vale Country Park

Getting there

From Junction 24 take the A57 Manchester. Enter Denton, and turn left at the traffic lights, Reddish Lane. Pass a station and enter Reddish. After a Morrisons turn left at the lights, Reddish Vale Road. Take the second entrance at the bottom of the hill, signed Country Park.

Return to M60 Junction 24

Leave the park. At the traffic lights, turn right B6167, Reddish Road. Continue to traffic lights and turn right, A57 Barnsley to return to the M60.

Walk

This is a wonderful walking park, and its wildness surprises, given that it lies in the middle of urban Manchester and a tangle of different motorways. Once a calico and dye works, the transformation into rural wonder is amazing.
There are a number of signed paths and routes through the park, with full details available from the visitor centre. Walks start across the bridge, and the paths are clear and well maintained.

Facilities

At the main entrance: free gated car park, WC+disabled, visitor centre, picnic area. Mobility scooter loan from the visitor centre, call 0161 4775637 to book. Campervan access.

M60 Junction 27

Eastbound only

Woodbank Memorial Park

Getting there

From Junction 27 take the A626 Marple. Turn left at the traffic lights, A626 Marple. Pass a Co-op supermarket, and turn left at traffic lights, Turncroft Lane. Park by the gates of the Vernon Museum Tea Rooms.

Return to M60 Eastbound

Return down Turncroft Lane and at the traffic lights turn right, Hall Street. At the next set of traffic lights turn right, signed M60. At the roundabout take exit 5, signed M60 East and rejoin the motorway.

Walk

There are two parks here, each with a distinctive character. Dog walkers will prefer the 90 acre Woodbank Memorial Park, which is cut through by a number of trails including the Fred Perry Way and the Valley Way. There's plenty of space here for off-lead walking and it seems that the further you go, the better it gets. To reach the Memorial Park, turn right at the sign by the entrance gates.

By contrast, Vernon Park is immaculately manicured, with display flowerbeds and gracious lawns.

Facilities

Free parking, disabled spaces. Tea Room 1000-1600 daily. Trail pack for walkers available from the museum. Campervan access.

M62

From Liverpool to Hull

Junction

M62 Junction 8

Clockface Colliery Country Park

Getting there

From Junction 8, turn to Burtonwood. Enter Burtonwood. Turn left, unsigned, Gorsey Lane. Pass a farm on the right and continue to a sign for Clockface Colliery country park. The unsigned entrance is on the left.

Return to M62 Junction 8

Turn right out of the car park. At the T-junction turn right, Clay Lane. At the roundabout take exit 2 signed M62 and return to the motorway.

Walk

This country park is a fantastic piece of regeneration work, transforming a former colliery site into a peaceful and spacious environment.
Popular with dog walkers and horse riders, there are many paths to wander along for a highly enjoyable walk. The paths are clear and wide, and there's no danger of getting lost. A real stressbuster of a park.

Facilities

Free car park, with height restriction, open 0800 to dusk.

WA5 9PB Sankey Valley Park

Getting there

From Junction 9 take the A49 Warrington. At a roundabout take exit 2, A574 Widnes and stay on the A574 Widnes over successive roundabouts until signed to Sankey Valley Park. Turn right to enter the park at a brown tourist sign.

Return to M62 Junction 9

Leave the park and take exit 3 at the roundabout, A574. At the next roundabout take exit 3, signed M62/M6 and continue through the roundabouts following signs to the M62.

Walk

Sankey Valley Park, part of the Mersey Forest, is a seven mile linear park, successfully created from a disused railway and waste ground. The Sankey Canal runs through the park. There is an emphasis on family pursuits, with a pirate ship and maze for children.

Signed pathways run through the park, and many other paths too. The canal path is ideal for dog walking and also forms part of the Trans-Pennine Trail. Once the choice is made to go left or right, the navigation couldn't be simpler.

Facilities

Free car park, WC+disabled (in visitor centre), visitor centre open 1200-1400, picnic area, children's activities and play areas. Campervan access.

M62 Junction 11

Risley Moss Nature Reserve *WA3 6QS*

Getting there

From Junction 11 take the A574 Warrington, eastbound exit 4, westbound exit 2. At a roundabout take exit 1, Risley Moss. At the next roundabout take exit 2, Risley Moss and enter the park from the next roundabout.

Return to M62 Junction 11

Exit the car park and at the roundabout take exit 2, signed M6, M62, Warrington. Continue straight at the next roundabout, and take exit 3 at the next roundabout A574, Manchester.

Continue on the A574 to return to the M62.

Walk

There are over 200 acres of natural space to enjoy at Risley Moss, with some well-signed trails as well as the opportunity to wander off-path and just soak up the surroundings.

An easy-access path is fully accessible and 650m.

The Nature Trail is 1.6km and leads through the trees on a well-maintained path.

Risley Moss is a site of special scientific interest because its peat has more or less survived industrialisation and marauding garden centres, and a regeneration project is underway to 're-wet' the peat.

Facilities

Car park free, gated. Visitor centre, WC, picnic tables, free dog poo bags from visitor centre. Campervan access.

OL16 3TD **Ogden Reservoir**

Getting there

From Junction 21 take exit 2, A663 Shaw. Turn left, A640 Huddersfield. Turn left, Ogden Lane, signed The Bull's Head.

Park in the car park opposite The Bull's Head.

Return to M62 Junction 21

Return down Ogden Lane and turn right at the T-junction. At the next junction turn right, Newhey Road, signed M62. Take exit 1 at a roundabout signed M62 and follow the signs to rejoin the motorway.

Walk

Turn left from the car park, and right up a lane (private road). Ahead and to the left you will see a green bank which forms the dam for Ogden Reservoir.

Turn left at a yellow waymark arrow to go up some steps and across the top of the dam. At the other side of the dam, climb the steps and turn right. Go through a kissing gate and continue ahead through a leafy landscape. Where the path forks, turn right to climb a small hill.

Near the top, there's a track and access to moorland with the opportunity to ramble for hours.

Facilities

At The Bull's Head (01706 847992), home made food. Dogs allowed in the beer garden. Closed Monday.

M62 Junction 22

Saddleworth Moor

Getting there

From Junction 22 take the A672 Oldham. Immediately after a 50mph sign pull into the car parking area on the right hand side.

Return to M62 Junction 22

Turn left out of the parking area and return to the M62.

Walk

This is part of the Pennine Way, so the scope for walking is limitless.

Cross the road and follow a path gently uphill through the moorland. The path is safe for off-lead dogs when you move away from the road, and there are wide open spaces to the left and right. Walk beyond the concrete trig point and turn around at your own halfway time.

There are also public footpath signs in the opposite direction.

Facilities

Free parking. Campervan access.

Oakwell Hall

Getting there
From Junction 27 take the A62, Huddersfield. Pass the West Yorkshire retail park/Ikea and continue at the traffic lights, signed Oakwell Hall Museum. At the next traffic lights turn right, Oakwell Hall Museum. Pass a pub on the left, and turn right into Oakwell Hall Country Park. Park in the Bottom car park.

Return to M62 Junction 27
Turn left out of the car park (Bottom car park). At the traffic lights turn left, signed M62 East and West and continue to rejoin the M62.

Walk
There are marked trails throughout the park, and detailed leaflets are available at the information point.
A well-planned system of paths makes the most of the 110 acres of the park. From the Bottom car park join the Nature trail (2 miles) to reach the visitor centre and facilities.
The focal point of the park is the Elizabethan manor house, featured in ITV's Wuthering Heights. The house museum is out of bounds for dogs, but the café is dog-friendly and provides large dog water bowls.

Facilities
Two free car parks, height restricted. WC+disabled, café, information point, shop, children's adventure playground and interactive activities, ranger service. Museum.

M62 Junction 36

Airmyn *DN14 8LD*

Getting there
From Junction 36 take the A614, Rawcliffe. Turn right, signed Airmyn. Enter the village and park in The Percy Arms car park.

Return to M62 Junction 36
Turn left out of the car park, and then left again onto the A614 to return to the motorway.

Walk
Cross the lane in front of the pub and up the steps onto a broad grassy pathway to the memorial and bear off into a field. The River Aire is to the left.
At the corner of the field it's possible to see where the Aire converges with the Ouse.
For a 40-50 minute walk, keep following the path around the fields alongside the river until your halfway point and then turn round to return to The Percy Arms.

Facilities
At the 17th century Percy Arms (01405 764408). Lunch served 1200-1400 Mon-Sat, Sun 1200-1700. Well-behaved dogs on leads are allowed in the bar, dog water is available.

Scotland

M8

Edinburgh to Greenock, via Glasgow

Junction

M9

Edinburgh to Stirling

M74 / A74M

Glasgow to Carlisle

M77
Glasgow to Fenwick

M90
Edinburgh to Perth

EH49 6PL Beecraigs Country Park

Getting there

From Junction 3 take the A899 Bathgate, Broxburn.
At the roundabout take exit 2, Dechmont A899 and at the following roundabout take exit 1, Dechmont. Turn right, Burnhouse Road, and continue for a mile. Turn left and pass Blackcraig Farm on the left, and then North Mains farm on the right. Turn right to enter Beecraigs Country Park.

Return to M8 Junction 3

Exit Beecraigs and turn left. Pass the farms and turn right, Burnhouse Road. At the T-junction turn left, and at the roundabout take exit 2, A899 and continue to return to the M8.

Walk

With over 900 acres of grounds, there is a real choice of walking routes in this very active country park. Choose your walk at the visitor centre and buy the route leaflet.
Three marked trails start from the Balvormie car park (turn left from the visitor centre car park, turn left and then left again). These are waymarked with coloured posts.
The Balvormie overflow car park is 20m beyond the entrance to the car park proper on the right. Don't be fooled by an apparently locked gate, the entrance is further on.

Facilities

Free parking. WC, visitor centre 0900-1600, shop, refreshments. Trail leaflets, 20p each. Rangers on duty. Partial wheelchair/buggy routes from some access points. Children's adventure playground. Dog water bowls. Campervan access.

Polkemmet Country Park *EH47 0AD*

Getting there

From Junction 5 merge onto the B7057 signed Shotts, Harthill.

At the T-junction turn left, B7066 Harthill. Enter Eastfield, pass a petrol station on the left, and enter West Lothian county.

Turn left at the tourist sign for Polkemmet Country Park.

Return to M8 Junction 5

Turn right out of the park, and turn right signed M8. Continue ahead and turn right, B7057, to return to the M8.

Walk

This country park has been formed from the grounds of the Baillie Estate.

There's a good choice of routes to suit all walkers' needs. The Red, Yellow and Blue routes are all under 2 miles, and the Green route is longer at just over 3 miles. There are also plenty of smaller paths to wander off on.

The Red and Blue routes start from the left of the car park entrance, and the Yellow and Green routes start just before the entrance to the car park.

As an extension to the red or blue trails, visit 'the Horn', a sculpture commissioned to liven up the view from the M8.

Facilities

Free parking. WC, children's playground and a steam train engine. Picnic tables and BBQ area. The children's 'Fantasy Forest' is off-limits to dogs. Campervan access.

EH49 7NG **Blackness Beach**

Getting there

From Junction 2 turn left, B8035 Forth Road Bridge. At a T-junction turn left, A904 Bo'ness and Blackness Castle. Turn right at a tourist sign to Blackness Castle. At a T-junction turn right and enter Blackness village. Turn left at the car park sign in the village and park in the sea-front car park.

Return to M9 Southbound

Leave the village on the B903, Linlithgow. At the T-junction turn left, A803 and continue to return to the M9 southbound.

Walk

Walk from the car park towards Blackness Castle and turn right at a footpath sign next to a dog bin. This is signed Chapel, and is a short circular walk route across headland meadows to the right of the castle complex. It's a good space for dogs and there's a grand view over the estuary to the Forth Bridge.

In fine weather a second option is to walk along the beach, away from the castle.

Blackness Castle, sitting squat and solid on its promontory, is mainly 16th century.

Facilities

At beach: free parking, WC. The Blackness Inn, snacks and bar meals, dogs allowed in the bar. Campervan access.

At Blackness Castle: WC, visitor centre, visitors' car park. Dogs on leads in courtyard only.

M9 Junction 3

Northbound only

Linlithgow Palace *EH49 7EY*

Getting there

From Junction 3 turn left, A803 Linlithgow. Enter Linlithgow and at the roundabout take exit 2, A803 Falkirk, Stirling and Linlithgow Palace. In the town centre turn right to Linlithgow Palace and car park.

Return to M9 Northbound

Exit Linlithgow Palace and turn right onto the A803. At the roundabout take exit 2 A803 and continue ahead to return to the M9.

Walk

For a short stroll, walk down the grassy slopes of the hill from the gatehouse, where there are several paths leading down to Linlithgow Loch. Turn right at the water and then amble around the base of the palace to return up the slope from the rear of the palace.

For a longer walk, follow the path down to the loch to a signed path around the loch.

The prosperous little town of Linlithgow has plenty of cafes and restaurants.

Facilities

Free parking. WC. Palace museum.

Tesco on the A803 roundabout for picnic supplies.

Getting there

From Junction 5 take exit 1 and follow signs to Falkirk A9. At Bog Roundabout take exit 1, A905 and at Mary Street Roundabout take exit 3, Falkirk A803. At the next roundabout turn left, Callendar House, and then right signed Callendar Park for the car park.

Return to M9 northbound

Leave the car park and cross the roundabout, signed M9. At the traffic lights turn right, signed M9. At the next roundabout continue ahead.

Follow the signs for M9 Grangemouth, to return to the M9 northbound.

Walk

At first this seems to be just a popular family park, where walkers and dogs take their chances with the youngsters enjoying the play facilities.

For a calm 40 minute walk aim for the lake, with the towers of Callendar House on the left, and make a circular tour of the lake, walking in a large area of stately parkland. Small paths lead off into light-dappled woodland, and dogs can run freely.

Facilities

Free car park. WC+disabled. Refreshments, kiosk for snacks, picnic tables. Children's play areas and swan pedaloes for hire on the lake. Dog poo bags available free from kiosk. Campervan access.

Bannockburn *FK7 OLJ*

Getting there

From Junction 9 follow the A872 Stirling, northbound exit 5, southbound exit 1. Follow the brown tourist signs to the Bannockburn Heritage Centre. The car park is on the left hand side, and clearly signed.

Return to M9 Junction 9

Turn right out of the car park, and follow signs to the M9.

Walk

If you first watch the bloodthirsty performance by the actor/warrior in the visitor centre the Bannockburn battlefield may be something of an anti-climax.

But the dog won't mind that the open land here is more playing field than ghost-filled museum, as it's an ideal space for a bound with the hound, or for young visitors brandishing swords.

Facilities

Free car park. Visitor centre 1000-1700, WC+disabled, shop, exhibition and exciting battle video. Campervan access.

Refreshments: motorway services at Junction 9; Klondike Garden Centre for coffee and cakes on the left before the entrance to Bannockburn, or the King Robert Hotel Bistro next to the battle site.

Getting there

From Junction 5 follow the tourist sign for Strathclyde Country Park. There are a number of car parks inside the park, all on the right hand side.

Return to M74 Junction 5 or 6

Northbound return to Junction 5: turn left from the car park and leave the park, continuing directly back to the M74 as signed.

Southbound return to Junction 6: turn right out of the car park and continue. At a crossroads turn right, drive over the river and follow signs to return to the M74 southbound.

Walk

Foreshaw beach, at the first car park, is popular with families and gives access to a grassy lakeside beach, children's playground, WC, and an ice-cream van in summer.

Scotland's first theme park, with cafes and children's entertainment, is on the left just before the second car park.

More rural walks start from the third or fourth car parks, where a number of trails lead down to the lakeside. A circular path is hard-surfaced, and accessible.

Facilities

Free parking. Campervan access.

Meals available at the Toby Carvery (in the Express Holiday Inn) just before the exit for M74 Junction 5.

M74 Junction 7

Southbound only

Chatelherault Country Park *ML3 7UE*

Getting there

Southbound access only

Leave the M74 at Junction 7 and turn right, Larkhall A72. Turn left at traffic lights, signed Chatelherault Country Park.

Return to M74 Southbound

Exit Chatelherault and turn left, A72. Continue until a right turn onto the A723. Follow signs to return to the M74 southbound.

Walk

There are six signed trails of different lengths around this 500 acre country park, and free leaflets for the 10 miles of trails can be picked up at the visitor centre. The Cadzow Oaks trail is one of the shorter walks, and The Riccarton Path is the longest of them all.

There is plenty of space at this fantastic park, and it's an ideal stopping point before heading into the city.

Facilities

Free parking, WC+disabled, café. First aid point. Exhibits and visitor centre. Children's adventure playground. Accessible paths. Big buckets of dog water. Campervan access.

Larkhall town has bakeries, several supermarkets and grocers for picnic provisions.

Castle Dangerous

Getting there

From Junction 12 take the A70 Ayr. Enter Douglas. Turn right at a brown sign to the Cameronian monument. Pass St Brides Church on the left, and park in a bay on the right opposite some cottages.

Return to M74 Northbound

Turn round and return along Main Street. Turn left at the T-junction and straight over a mini-roundabout. At the roundabout take exit 1, A70 Edinburgh. At the next roundabout take exit 1, Glasgow M74.

Walk

Leave the parking area and follow the black footpath arrow along the track to Castle Dangerous, past a lake on the left. Return the same way.

Earlier castles here enjoyed a brutal and gory past defending the route to the Clyde Valley, and the Heritage Centre in the town has the full details.

Facilities

Free parking. Campervan access. Picnic tables on the walk route. Hard tarmac path (after cattle grid). Children's playground in park below church. Shops in the town for picnic supplies, and petrol station.

A74 (M) Junction 15

Moffat

Getting there

From Junction 15 follow signs to Moffat A701. Enter Moffat and park in the first car park on the left.

Return to A74(M) Junction 15

Turn right out of the car park, and continue on the A701 to rejoin the motorway.

Walk

Branded as the first 'Walkers Town' in Scotland, some real passion has gone into creating walking trails in and around Moffat.

Trails start at the car park and include a 2 mile walk to Chapel, and a Woodside walk at around 3 miles.

Many paths are hard-surfaced, and fully accessible to wheelchairs and buggies.

Longer routes include woodland walks (Gallowhill), and a forest walk in Craigieburn (just over 6 miles). Only one walk may have dog restrictions due to cattle grazing.

There are many more walks, and a walking festival in October.

Facilities

Free parking. WC. Board with walking trail routes. Shops for picnic supplies. Campervan access.

Meals served at The Black Bull Hotel (01683 220206; DG10 9EG), and The Buccleigh Arms Hotel (01683 220003; DG10 9ET). Well-behaved dogs are welcome in both hotels.

DG11 2RG Lockerbie Manor Hotel

Getting there

From Junction 17 follow signs for Lockerbie B7068. At the next roundabout take the Lockerbie B7068 exit and turn left. At a T-junction turn left, and turn right to park at the Lockerbie Manor Hotel (patrons only).

Return to A74(M) Junction 17

Turn left at the end of the hotel drive. Take the first right turn, unsigned. Cross a light controlled bridge, and then turn right at a T-junction. Thereafter the A74(M) is signed.

Walk

This walk lies within the extensive grounds of the hotel, and is a safe space for children and dogs to let off steam.
Walk slightly downhill with the hotel to the left. Go through a gate, ignoring a path to the right. Turn right at the path junction and then right onto a narrower path before a white cottage. The path seems overgrown at this point, but opens out past a 5-bar gate to cross a stream. Continue uphill for a while, and then turn round to return to the hotel.

Facilities

At the Lockerbie Manor Hotel (01576 202610): coffee, meals, tea, in old-style, relaxing comfort. Well-behaved dogs on leads are permitted in the lounge, dog water provided. Campervan access.

A74 (M) Junction 18

Northbound only

Lochmaben Castle

Getting there

From Junction 18 turn right B723, Lockerbie. Bear left, B7076 and take exit 2 at a roundabout. Turn right, Lockerbie, and at a T-junction turn right, Lochmaben A709. Enter Lochmaben and turn left, Dalton B7020. Turn left signed Lochmaben Castle and park by the castle ruins.

Return to A74(M) Northbound

Leave the castle and turn right at the end of the track. Enter Lochmaben and turn right at the T-junction, signed A709 Lockerbie. Turn left, signed A74(M) and at the next roundabout turn right. Follow the signs back to the A74(M) North.

Walk

For a shortish walk, take the grassy path running anti-clockwise around the lake.

Close by the castle is a small 'beach', ideal for dog swimming, and also picnic tables. Longer walks are signed from the track to the castle, and signed with green pointers.

The castle has seen a lot of action over the centuries. It was owned at one time by the Brus family, ancestors of the famous Bruce.

Facilities

Free parking. Picnic tables.

Brownmoor Wood

Getting there

From Junction 19 take the B725 Ecclefechan, exit 1 at the roundabout. At the next roundabout, take exit 1 Ecclefechan B7076. Turn right onto a minor road and pass the entrance to the Cressfield Caravan Park. Continue to the end and park.

Return to A74(M)

Return down the lane and turn left. At a roundabout take exit 2, A74(M) and return to the motorway.

Walk

Walk past a bungalow to a clear path and through three swing gates towards the woodland ahead. Pass a Brownmoor Wood Forestry Commission sign, and stay on the path as it winds gently uphill. After 100m or so there is a clearing, and the start point of two marked circular trails in the forest, one red coded and the other blue coded. The paths are well maintained and easy to follow.

The essayist and historian Thomas Carlyle was born and raised in Ecclefechan. He was buried in the churchyard here, after refusing a berth at Westminster Abbey.

Facilities

Free parking. Picnic tables. Campervan access. Public WC in Ecclefechan. Coffee and food at the Creswell Court House Hotel, no dogs permitted.

Pollok House and Country Park

Getting there
From Junction 2 follow the sign for Pollokshaws B762. At the Round Toll roundabout take exit 1 Pollokshaws B769. Follow the B769 and turn left at a sign for Pollok House and Country Park. The car park is just after the entrance to Pollok House.

Return to M77 Junction 2
Follow the one-way system to leave the park at the Dumbreck Road exit. Turn right onto the B769. At the Round Toll roundabout take exit 3 signed M77 and return to the motorway.

Walk
A marked trail explores the 360 acres of parkland, and some of the historical, natural and manmade features of the park. There is a small area surrounding the house where dogs must be on leads, but otherwise the grounds are open to unfettered canine exploration. Highland Cattle live in the grounds and wise walkers will avoid upsetting them.

Facilities
Free car park. Disabled parking places outside Pollok house museum. WC+disabled in Old Stable Yard and Burrell Collection, tea rooms, children's play area. Dog water. Full access to house and park for disabled visitors. Campervan access.

Getting there

From Junction 3 take the A907, Dunfermline. Pass a football ground. At the next roundabout take the A907 Stirling, Pittencrieff Park. Turn left, signed Tourist Information, and park in the Glenbridge short stay car park on the left.

Return to M90 Junction 3

Leave the car park and turn right at the traffic lights. Carry straight on to rejoin the M90.

Walk

Follow the blue signs to enter Pittencrieff Park. Inside the park waymarked trails wander through the 76 acres of the park, past formal gardens, an ornamental waterfall, and museum.

Other visitor attractions are near the park gates on the other side.

Facilities

P&D car park. Campervan access.

In Pittencrieff Park: WC+disabled, restaurant, hard surface paths, dog exercise area, children's play areas.

In Dunfermline: cafes, restaurants and pubs, many with outdoor seating. Plenty of bakeries and delis for picnic supplies.

Lochore Meadows *KY5 8BA*

Getting there
Follow signs to Glenrothes B9097. At a T-junction turn right, B966 Cowden Heath. Turn left, Ballingry, Lochore. Enter Ballingry. Turn right at a T-junction. Enter Crosshill. Turn right, signed Lochore Meadows Country Park. The car park is at the end of the lane.

Return to M90 Junction 5
Leave the park, turn left at the mini-roundabout. Turn left, Ballingry Road and at the T-junction turn left. Turn right, B996 then left, B9097 to return to the M90.

Walk
There are four marked trails in this extensive country park.
The Golden Triangle walk is wheelchair accessible, and is a mile long hard path to a castle and back.
A three mile circular path around the loch is also hard surfaced.
The third trail is an uphill track to Harran Woods, and the final choice 'The Pit Road' is a 3 mile flat path winding around the headstocks of a former coal mine. Other woodland paths are signed in red.
Dogs should be taken to use the dog loop before starting a walk.

Facilities
Free parking. WC+disabled. Visitor centre 1000-1600. Also WCs at the Outdoor Centre when the visitor centre is closed. Café. Ranger service. Children's play area, boats and a small beach for families (no dogs on the beach). Campervan access.

Getting there

From Junction 6 take the A977 Kinross. Continue to the B918 (Station Road) and at a mini roundabout turn right. Turn left at a sign to Lochleven Castle, and follow signs for the castle through a residential area and then park near the Boathouse Bistro.

Return to M90 Junction 6

Turn right at the end of Burns Begg Street. At a mini-roundabout turn left, Station Road and return to the M90.

Walk

Take the ducted path opposite the Bistro to the Loch Leven nature reserve. Kids will head off to the pirate playground on the left while keen swimming hounds will be equally intent on getting to one of the lochside dog beaches. The path follows a line of sight to the trees and the small promontory directly ahead, just under a mile

Boats go to the Lochleven island castle, where Mary Queen of Scots was once a 'guest'.

Facilities

Free car park. WC. Picnic tables at the park. Campervan access.

All day meals are available at the Boathouse Bistro (01577 865386).

Scone Palace *PH2 6BD*

Getting there
From Junction 11 take the A85 Perth. Enter Perth and follow signs to Blairgowrie. Turn left, A93 Blairgowrie and Scone Palace. Turn left into Scone Palace when signed.

Return to M90 Junction 11
Leave the palace grounds and turn right. Continue at the traffic lights, and follow the blue signs to return to the M90.

Walk
A grand location for a walk, combining a visit to one of Scotland's premier visitor spots with fun activities for kids, historical viewing underpinned by a fine coffee shop, tasteful souvenir shopping, and dog happiness too.
Turn right to pass through the gateway opposite the palace and this will bring you into The Wild Garden and Pinetum, ideal for a short walk where dogs can run off-lead.

Facilities
Grounds entry £4.80, RHS free. Open 0900-1700. WC+disabled. Shop, restaurant and café with outdoor seating. Children's activities. House, Gallery, Museum. Dog water at café. Campervan access.